A SHORT BORDER HANDBOOK

A Journey Through the Immigrant's Labyrinth

To Serge and Yelena
many happy Thanksgiving
together

A SHORT BORDER HANDBOOK

A Journey Through the Immigrant's Labyrinth

Gazmend Kapllani

Translated from the Greek by Anne-Marie Stanton-Ife

New Europe Books

Williamstown, Massachusetts

Published by New Europe Books
Williamstown, Massachusetts
www.NewEuropeBooks.com
Copyright © 2017 by Gazmend Kapllani
English translation © 2017 by Anne-Marie Stanton-Ife
Interior design by Knowledge Publishing Services

Previously published in English in 2010 by Portobello Books Ltd,
Twelve Addison Avenue, Holland Park, London.
First published in Greece by Livanis Publishers.
This edition is published by arrangement with Ampi Margini Literary
Agency, London, www.ampimargini.com.

ISBN: 978-0-9973169-8-8

Cataloging-in-Publication Data is available from the Library of
Congress.

First US edition

10 9 8 7 6 5 4 3 2 1

For my mother, Qerime.

For my father, Myrteza.

For my brother, Artionil.

Prologue

I'm not crazy about borders; I can't honestly say I hate them, either. It's just that they scare me, that's all, and I always feel uncomfortable when I get too close to one. Let's get something straight: I'm talking about visible borders here, geographical borders, the ones that mark off one country from another, one state from another, one nation from another. Even today, as they become increasingly porous, whenever I cross one I get a very strange feeling, a mixture of deliverance and perplexity. Perhaps it's because of my passport. I've got used to that suspicious look they give me. I return it with one of longing, and impatience to get to the other side; but it's no use, it's almost invariably met with hostility and suspicion. I do try to reassure them, try to persuade them that I represent no danger of any kind, but there always seems to be some pretext or other for rebuffing me, some excuse for not treating me as an equal. This is why I say I suffer from Border Syndrome, and have done for a long time. Border Syndrome is a form of illness that's difficult to describe with precision. Unlike agoraphobia or depression, it doesn't feature on the list of recognized mental disorders. But what I can do, perhaps a little later, is outline some of the main symptoms. I do know that there are other sufferers, a great many of them. Those who have never experienced the urge to cross a border, or who have never experienced rejection at a border, will have a hard time understanding us.

My difficult relationship with borders goes back a very long way, back to my childhood, because whether or not you end up with Border Syndrome is largely a matter of luck: it depends on where you're born.

I was born in Albania.

1

*R*eaching, never mind crossing, the borders of a country under a totalitarian regime like Albania was, until 1991, the equivalent of a miracle—or a mortal sin. Exit visas were few and far between; those who got them were the lucky ones. The rest of us, most of us, that is, looked on the ones who got them as a breed apart, something along the lines of extraterrestrials. We were condemned to speculate endlessly about what lay on the other side of the borders. Either that or we would torture ourselves with the simple conclusion that life went on as normal, even on the other side.

Dismissing the possibility that there was life beyond the borders proved quite an effective survival strategy, spiritually as well as physically. At some point, in the subconscious of many of us, the world-beyond-the-borders became more than the continuation in time and space of some common world.

As the years went by, and Albania's isolation became absolute, the world-beyond-the-borders gradually assumed the status of a separate planet. For some people that planet was paradise, for others it was a place of terror. But for all that, another planet.

Why are you telling us all this?
You could ask the immigrant, Why are you telling us all this? The truth is, as an immigrant, especially a first-generation immigrant, your first instinct is to stay silent. Fear; caution; the violent escape, that violent first encounter with the unknown country; that feeling

of being uninvited; resentment; longing for and rejection of home, and guilt and rage at the same time, all take root in the immigrant. An immigrant is a confused creature, highly insecure, and that is why he fears confession. All it takes is one gesture from the other side, one sign of denial, or indifference, of the "What's it to me where you come from and what you've been through?" kind, for the immigrant to feel ridiculous, vulnerable, and freakish. That's why he doesn't take risks. Instead, he digests his experiences in isolation and before long is convinced that they are of absolutely no interest to anyone. In the final analysis, he thinks: I wasn't made for telling stories, but to fight tooth and nail for my survival. It's not that people can't understand; they just don't want to.

The alternative, baring all and confessing, is risky. Telling his life story, the painful and contradictory journey of an immigrant. But, if he keeps it all bottled up inside, he is in danger of becoming neurotic and resentful. The most he can hope for is that they will understand, first him, and then all those who cannot speak, who don't know how to speak, who don't have the courage to speak and who bury their narratives deep inside themselves instead. You cannot understand an immigrant if you haven't heard his story first.

2

The regime did everything in its power to block all images from the other side of the border by means of controls, arrests, and punishments. I can still remember—I was in the second year of primary school at the time—the day the school's Party secretary walked into our classroom and, among other things, asked us in a ponderous voice (which, with monumental exertion, she tried to soften) if our parents watched anything apart from Albanian state television. With the naiveté of a child wanting to impress his classmates, I stuck my hand up and duly announced that my parents enjoyed watching a channel called Savra. There was no such thing; Savra was the name of a village near our town, Lushnjë. But I didn't know that. My father, alert to the dangers involved, dealt with my unfettered childish curiosity by feeding it with certain pseudonyms and code words for the foreign television stations he watched on the quiet. Ultimately, not even that could save him. That evening, he was summoned to the headmaster's office and asked to account for this unknown television station. You could lose your job over something like that—and that was the least of it. He risked being accused of "reactionary activities" and of harboring "petit bourgeois sympathies" and risked being tried for disseminating antistate propaganda. After that, he could end up in one of those terrifying jails for political prisoners, or else be sent to one of those villages outside Lushnjë that were full of exiles. Savra was the best known. The truth was that there were options *at their disposal for finishing someone off. My father had to explain himself, and explain why, first of all, he did not restrict his viewing to Albanian state television, and why he moved around in wealthy capitalist-imperialist-revisionist-Titoist-monarcho-fascist etc., etc. circles. Secondly, he was required to account for his choice of pseudonym. Why Savra? Did this imply indirect yet unambiguous sympathy for the enemies of the state exiled in that village? He answered flatly that he did not watch foreign television, adding that if they didn't believe him, they were welcome to come and inspect the antenna on his roof.*

On the subject of antennas, all citizens were required by the regime to purchase special ones, which had to be installed in such a way as if to renounce any desire to receive images from the world-beyond-the-borders. The truth was that my father had two antennas: one on the roof, for appearances' sake, and another, illegal one, the one referred to inside the family as "the antlers." It was an indoor antenna, used mainly for picking up Italian channels. This double antenna was the perfect symbol for the divided individual living in a totalitarian state. One side of you functioned to appease the terrifying gaze of the regime; the other, more congenial side tried to escape its all-powerful watch by cunning.

Fortunately the episode with the antenna did not have further repercussions. I was treated to a stinging slap from my father, sealing my hatred for the Party secretary, and although still a child, I began to realize that I had to stop being one, especially when it came to dealing with Party secretaries. I was so furious with her that I secretly prayed that some terrible fate would befall her, as that, and only that, would assuage my wrath, and only then in part. I wished—fantasized even—about her slipping, falling, and breaking her leg—both legs; that she would fall ill and die a slow, painful death; that a brick would land on her head, killing her on the spot. The fantasy that brought me absolute satisfaction, however, was seeing her lying on the ground, squashed under the wheels of a cart (one of those from the farmers' cooperative, on filthy wheels pulled by emaciated horses that you used to see driving around town).

Time passed and with it my sadistic fantasies. I found out, much later, that my prayers had been answered in part, but not quite in the way I'd imagined: the Party secretary developed a peculiar illness, which made her look permanently cheerful. It was unbelievable considering she was one of the most stony-faced people on the planet. At school she was known as "the statue." Now each time there was a Party convention, she would collapse in fits of laughter, shrieking away, and the more she shrieked, the more idiotic she looked. News of her nervous laughter reached the Party Committee, which ruled that in the interests of ideology, the Party, and the revolution she should go into early retirement. As they pointed out, she was not simply unsuitable but was harming the revolution and the dictatorship of the proletariat through her infirmity. That was the last she was heard of.

Leaving your country means breaking with it.

A true emigrant is an incorrigible, egotistical narcissist. He thinks he's too good for his native land, and does not deserve the poverty, the lack of prospects, the violence, the corruption, the filth, the hypocrisy, or the lack of love. For all these reasons, for him, exile is above all a choice.

Leaving is a choice, a choice to break with the country of his birth. This break follows him for the rest of his life. It will be the source of his sense of guilt and of freedom, rejection and denial, daydreaming and nostalgia, forgetting and melancholy, mood swings and schizophrenia. Only if he makes a success of life abroad, only then can he make peace with his own country again. If he doesn't make it, he will be left hanging, at odds with the world and with the universe. He will make a great show of how much he loves his country of origin for one reason alone—to annoy people in his new country, the country he believed would offer him a better future, but which, in his opinion, has denied him one. In the final analysis, he has rejected his own country in favor of this new one; he has had more faith in this new one than in his own. Shouldn't that in itself be enough for them to hold their doors wide open for me? he asks himself.

3

*T*hose antennas will always be connected in my mind with two more people who made a lasting impression on me during my childhood: Uncle Jani and comrade Mete. I had known Uncle Jani almost all my life because we lived in the same block. His flat was upstairs from us, on the fourth floor. He was quite well known around town, mainly because he waged an undeclared war on all enemies of the state and the revolution, the enemy without, certainly, but especially the enemy within. From the conversations of the grown-ups at home and at friends' homes, I learned that Uncle Jani had an enormous logbook, which he kept hidden somewhere in his flat, detailing the works and days of all suspect residents of our town. Woe betide anyone whose name appeared on the list; it meant certain ruin for them and their relatives. Rumors about Uncle Jani's list grew until it acquired mythical status within the community. Some said that it was just a simple notebook; others maintained it was a huge tome containing information relating not only to suspect persons in this town but in the neighboring one, too. Uncle Jani was so committed to hunting down the enemy within that it was said that even his daughter-in-law's name appeared on the list. They all lived under the same roof. One night, he overheard her talking in her sleep, murmuring, "I don't give a shit about the Party conference…."

Irrespective of how long or how short Uncle Jani's list really was, the fact was that nobody in our block suffered at his hands, except Keme's son, *that is. Rolling home drunk one night, he had the misfortune of falling across Uncle Jani, who fixed him with a stern gaze. Keme's son, who worked as a porter, returned Uncle Jani's look with these words: "They say that drunkards lose all sense of smell—even so, I couldn't fail to sniff out a filthy informer like you!" before collapsing into fits of laughter. He lost his job because of it, but everyone said he'd got off very lightly and that Uncle Jani had proved that he did have a human side, because if he'd really wanted to, he could have had Keme's son exiled or even thrown into prison.*

Uncle Jani was not the only one targeting the enemy within. There were others in town doing the very same thing. We knew about some of them, but not all. Comrade Mete, for example, we did not know about. We only found out about him much later, under the most tragic circumstances. Comrade Mete's particular skill and passion was tracking down the enemy within through the precise study of the lie of their television antennas. He left no rooftop in the town uninspected at least three or four times, operating under cover of night to make sure the direction of all antennas conformed to Party regulations. In fact he had compiled a long list of names next to which was recorded the direction of the lie of their antennas. If Comrade Mete discovered an aberration anywhere, the authorities were alerted instantly and the guilty party could find himself digging trenches for years on end. Comrade Mete's legendary list was discovered late one night on the roof of our block. Unfortunately the owner of the list was five floors away from it, lying on the ground at the entrance to the building, having executed the most spectacular fall from the roof, all the way down to the ground below, which was still damp from the recent rain. Comrade Mete's fall was accompanied by a terrible scream that sent a jolt through everyone in our building, waking everyone in the surrounding blocks as well. Comrade Mete died on impact. A tragic, premature death, but a hero's death; he was killed in the line of duty, fighting for socialism and in the class struggle. What caused his fall, however, was never established, and speculation concerning the mysterious circumstances surrounding his demise continued to fuel the imaginations of the people of our town.

The Immigrant in the Realm of the Imperative

You have to get a job. Any job. You have to survive. You have to find somewhere to live—doesn't matter what it's like as long as it looks vaguely like a home. You have to learn the language, even if you can't understand a single word of it and you get your "good nights" and your "good evenings" all mixed up. You have to learn to speak more softly, and not shout, because it scares people. You're not back home in the village now, you know. You have to keep out of the way of those Black Marias because you turned up in this country without an invitation, making quite an entrance with that woebegone expression of yours and that primitive haircut. People round here haven't seen anything like that for decades, especially not combined with those clothes, so obviously charity clothes—or maybe you stole them? You have to learn how to walk properly because you've got used to walking too fast, like you've got the Devil on your back. You've got to learn the Highway Code, the sections that apply to pedestrians of course, and you've got to stop looking at all those gorgeous local girls like that, the way Quasimodo looks at Esmeralda in Notre Dame de Paris. You have to, have to, have to...without end or expiry date. Day after day, night after night, week after week, month after month, year after year. Not for you the privilege of wanting—you are condemned to live by the mercilessly cruel claims of "have to." Because you have to make it. Above all, make it.

This is the immigrant's oath.

Just as doctors are supposed to live by the Hippocratic oath, an immigrant lives by "I have to succeed." This oath is his only real country from now on. He has to make it, not simply because people back home expect something from him; that's the least of it. He has to make it because he cannot go back a failure. The thought of failure makes him tremble like a child afraid of the dark. He has to make it, but how? And this is where the common path of immigrants diverges and they split off into successes and failures, the accepted and the rejected, the lucky and the unlucky. Because immigrants, whatever their superficial similarities, differ from each other in exactly the way that everybody in this world differs from everybody else.

4

*T*here were two basic versions of how comrade Mete met his death. The first version circulated in hushed tones and low voices from house to house and café to café. The story went that comrade Mete, in addition to his weakness for television antennas, was victim of another obsession, much, much stranger than the first. A committed voyeur, he lived to watch couples in the throes of lovemaking, longed for glimpses of women hitching up their skirts to reveal their naked backsides when visiting the toilet or getting into the bath. That fateful night, it was rumored, he was spying on the female judge who lived in the top floor flat in our building, while she was having her bath, and he was completely mesmerized by her ample backside. Completely in the thrall of his passion, and in his efforts not to miss a single ounce of the pleasure this sight brought him, he had balanced himself precariously, giving scant attention to his calculation of the angle. Unfortunately for him, it had been raining, that's why he slid off, losing at once both his view of the judge's backside and his life. That at least is what those loyal to the first version claimed.

The second version was the one championed by Uncle Jani. According to him, comrade Mete was the victim of a conspiracy of enemies within. He swore that he would find the enemy behind this treacherous murder, the heroic death of comrade Mete, if it was the last thing he did. One day he announced that his investigations had progressed, and the enemy within was in fact within our own building.

His news spread panic through the block. Keme, because his son had been in trouble with Uncle Jani, was worried that Uncle Jani had him on his list as a main suspect, and for that reason sold his television to limit the risk of being accused of watching foreign television stations. Another neighbor, Loni, was in the hospital being treated for severe psychological disorders following a nightmare in which Uncle Jani forced him to dig up comrade Mete's body. Uncle Jani, however, died of a sudden heart attack. His death was greeted by several people in the building with sighs of relief. Behind closed doors, of course.

A Hero Verging on the Ridiculous

There is something heroic about the way an immigrant abandons his native land. Nevertheless, in his everyday life, he is fragile, confused, and at times ridiculous, like a card player who dreams of that one amazing trick but lacks essential knowledge of the rules of the game. He thought that he had arrived in a place where everything would be easy, where help would be at hand, where people would explain the rules to him, and not only that, would praise him if he managed to beat them. Now he discovers that his idols don't give a damn about him; he discovers something worse, that no one asked him to come, that he is there uninvited, and nobody notices him. An invisible creature, which, on the rare occasions it is noticed, inspires either momentary pity or lasting disgust.

If only he knew the language, he thinks, he would show all those people who are unworthy to so much as look at him. They need to be shown how much he is worth, and that is a great deal. But he doesn't know the language, and he is terrified, because these locals speak so quickly—it's like listening to a sewing machine. No, there's no way he's going to learn it. They can go hang, the lot of them, and take their language with them. But if he doesn't learn it, how is he going to find a job?

How will he survive? Just the basics then, the first ten words. And he does manage to learn them even though he's not quite sure how. That's when he discovers that this language isn't as impossible as he'd thought. It starts to grow on him. He speaks it and is no longer just some mute presence. But this enthusiasm is short-lived. In his hands, the language is not spoken but broken. He doesn't just break it, he butchers it. Feminine names become masculine, masculine feminine, and most nouns are neutered. Better mute than annoying.

5

All of this was going on at a time when the regime decreed Albania the rose garden and solitary beacon of hope in the universe. Our teachers at school told us over and over again that we were something like the chosen people. And, if you number among the elect, two things are required of you: first, you have to hate the nonelect; second, you must at all costs be happy. Happiness in a totalitarian regime is not a question of choice or fortune; it is a duty. Public displays of unhappiness were viewed with suspicion.

The point was that we were the only happy people, the only genuinely happy people, the only pure, the only victims, while against us were the miserable, the liars, primitive and polluted predators. Sometimes I used to think that we Albanians had hit something like a Universal Jackpot of Fortune: all the happiness, the authenticity, the purity, of the universe was contained within a mere 28,000 square kilometers, the surface area of Albania.

In our minds, the world was divided into two—Paradise (us) and Hell (everyone else), and whoever tried to cross the borders of paradise and escape was automatically branded Hell's accomplice. For that reason, passports were abolished as we had no use for them, and attempts to escape from Albania were considered high treason.

One fine day, however, in my childhood innocence, the borders invaded the world of my imagination in the bloodiest way conceivable.

The death of my neighbor, Artur, brought them to life for me like the most terrifying ghosts.

If you were a tourist ...

If you were a tourist, your broken Greek would endear you to people. When it comes down to it, this is the real difficulty about difference: when an American speaks broken Greek, he is classed as a "nice American," but when an Albanian speaks broken Greek, he is classed as nothing more than a "bloody Albanian." When an American speaks perfect Greek, he is an "exceptional American," but when an Albanian speaks perfect Greek, all he hears is, "You'll never be Greek! You'll never be Greek!"

Since he is nothing more than a pitiful illegal immigrant, his broken Greek gets on the nerves of the locals. And he knows it. Because of this, every time he gets on the bus, he speaks in a low voice, avoids conversation, and sweats with embarrassment when people try to speak to him because as soon as the locals catch his accent, they turn away and he feels like he's suddenly been struck by avian flu.

How did it happen, he asks himself, *why do they look at me with such fear?* He would like to ask them, "What are you all so afraid of?—I love this country." But he doesn't ask, because he already knows the answer. "Don't you watch the news? You lot have taken over this country, you lot have slaughtered us in our beds: they should round you all up, the lot of you, and take you back to where you came from. Back to your own bloody country." *So soon!* he says to himself. *They can't send me back so soon. I've only just found a job. And I work like a dog, night and day, in wind and rain. Look at my hands, they look like someone's been hacking them with a sword. I work to spare your hands. I want to buy a car too. No, I'll start off with a big stereo, then I'll get a huge color TV, then a big washing machine, and then, I don't know, we'll see.*

And at that moment he realizes that he is upset, that the phrase "your own bloody country" has got to him. Of course he's familiar with all the shit there, which is why he left in the first place, but it's not a "bloody country." There are small children there, just like here; there are mothers who love their children there, just like here; there are teenagers falling in love back there, just like here; there are those who hope and those who despair just like here—though the truth is that those who despair now outnumber those who hope.

The bus suddenly stops and two men get on. They are wearing identical uniforms and identical grim expressions. His blood freezes. "Illegal immigrants—out, out, out!" Then "Down, down, down, down!" And he gets down, down, down, further down all the time until he can't go any lower. Fuck.

6

*T*hat was when the Chinese arrived. It was as though they had fallen from the sky, peacefully invading our town. We woke up one morning and there they were. We saw them and they saw us. There were dozens of them, all dressed in identical blue uniforms, walking hurriedly around, Mao's Little Red Book in hand. Albania was in the throes of a passionate love affair with China. We all looked on, at a loss to understand what they were doing here. Rumors and speculation were rife in the cafés and in the conversations of the adults. The townspeople, although they admitted that they could not tell one Chinese person from the next, because they looked like identical twins, even started to learn a few Chinese names and words.

Some said that the Chinese had come to open a factory producing military aircraft; and others, blessed with even more fertile imaginations, claimed that they had come to transform Albania into the biggest industrialized nation in Europe. In the end it turned out that they had come simply to build a plastics factory just outside town.

As for our teachers, they informed us that we no longer had to fear any enemy, as Mao Zedong had given his word to Enver Hoxha that if anyone dared lay a finger on Albania, one billion Chinese would came running to its defense. In other words, this small nation of three million, given its friendship with China, should now be considered to have a population of 1,300,000,000.

The most dramatic scene of our encounter with the Chinese played out one morning as they filled the small square in front of the town's only hotel, where they were all staying. They were making strange movements, something like a slow-motion version of ballet. Each was in his own world; some were shaking their heads, others moving their hands, some were kneeling slowly down, others were slowly raising their knees up to their chests. They were all dressed in blue and looked absolutely mad. We hadn't a clue what they were doing; almost the entire town had gathered around the square to gawk at the Chinese, to the point that the police grew worried at the size of the crowd. Then all of a sudden we were told that they were just taking exercise, which prompted such comments from the crowd as, "Allah, preserve us from these people."

*

I mention the Chinese simply because Artur left a few weeks after their arrival, in December, round about New Year's Eve, for a village on the way to Korçë, near the borders. He had an aunt living there and wanted to see in the New Year with her. In those days, in order to get to those border villages, you had to have a special permit from the police, as these villages fell in the designated "forbidden zone."

It later turned out that Artur had not gone to his aunt's house with the intention of spending the New Year with her at all; he wanted to escape. He had calculated, at least that's what people said after the funeral, that the soldiers on the borders would be more relaxed and less vigilant over the holiday season than at other times. He was wrong. The soldiers spotted him trying to escape and shot him dead. I later found out that a soldier responsible for killing someone trying to escape was rewarded with a few days' paid leave. The thought of those soldiers sitting around arguing over who was entitled to the time off made my skin crawl.

Artur's death shocked me deeply. It also fired my imagination, and gradually the borders took on metaphysical proportions for me. They haunted my sleep, and nothing pleased me more during my waking hours than listening to stories that were in some way connected to borders: arrests, killings, attempted escapes which had mostly failed.

To me the few who managed to get out were the strongest, most special people in the entire world. Some were even from our town. Everyone knew about them, not just because they'd escaped, but because of the repercussions and the terror that followed. Their families were sent into exile; their relatives lost their jobs, forever stigmatized for having an "enemy of the people" in their family. Of course, their relatives automatically came under suspicion themselves, suspected enemies of the people forever, on a par with the lepers of the Middle Ages, and were favorite targets of the stool pigeons who had infested our lives.

Crossing Illegally, Again and Again

He will cross back again, go back into Greece. Korçë–Kalabaka[1], eight days on foot, nights spent under the stars, if they are out, that is. The "guide," who knows his way through all those hidden paths, charges $300 a head. A typical group of illegals ranges from eight to eleven heads. Bargaining starts in Korçë, the guarantor holds the money, and if they're caught by soldiers and sent back, everybody gets their money back. That's the deal, at any rate, but you never know, because frequently the guarantor vanishes into thin air and the illegals are left with nothing more than a bitter taste in their mouths. But he will cross the mountains again, back into Greece. They might catch him again in six months' time in almost exactly the same way. The two men wearing identical uniforms and identical grim expressions will get on the bus again. This will be followed by: Black Maria. Holding cell, crowded: five people in a two by two cell. Prisoners arguing, the stench of piss—a completely shit existence. He will wait a few days, until enough people have been rounded up for transportation up to the borders, and the Black Maria will drive them up to Kakavia.[2] At the border he will get on a truck that will take him back to the village. He'll be greeted with a "Get caught again, did you?" from his relatives, while the villagers snidely remark, "Get caught again, did he? Poor bastard. Not surprising. Takes guts to live so far away from home."

7

A large country—Russia, for example—isolated with hermetically sealed borders is like one endless prison, but tiny Albania, also isolated with hermetically sealed borders, is more like a regular straitjacket.

When I was in high school, my friends and I (or at least the few people I dared reveal my thoughts to) used to say that if you wanted to see the borders of the motherland, all you had to do was climb up onto the roof of a block of flats.

I remember our school trip to Sarandë, where at night you can see the lights from the world-beyond-the-borders. They might have been the lights from a village, maybe a town, who knows? We stood there, gawking at them, imagining, speculating, in secret: "What are people like on the other side?" We each had our own ideas on the subject, usually the product of rumors, or pictures we'd seen on television, transformed into mythical stories, which we'd use to feed our fantasies as much as we could. We talked about beautiful beaches, swimming pools, color TVs, but most of all about gorgeous girls, hampered neither by excess pounds nor sexual restraint.

"Girls there are liberated; they don't expect you to come on to them, they do all the work," one of my friends reliably informed us. "They're free out there, how can I put it? You're constantly ambushed by sex!" he continued, placing unbearable pressure on our adolescent fantasies.

At that moment, one of the girls in our class, a brilliant but hopelessly naïve student, asked our instructor in Marxist-Leninism to explain why capitalist cities were so well-illuminated when the proletariat living there was supposedly dying of starvation in dark slums. The teacher looked down at her over the top of his spectacles, and let his eyes roam across the entire class. As soon as he'd reassured himself that the question was motivated by nothing more than innocent curiosity, he answered with his customary ease, the style he used when he explained that in the capitalist West, the proletariat works a twenty-hour day, sustained only by a diet of boiled greens. "It looks to me as if some of you have been up till all hours staring at Greek monarcho-fascist lighting instead of getting a good night's sleep to wake refreshed to face the class enemy. Well, let me tell you, the lights you saw come from the villas of the rich. They live in enormous houses while the workers starve, the workers have nothing. They live in darkness, unlike the happy proletariat in our country. Read over the notes you take from my talks, and you'll sleep better at night, untroubled by reactionary doubts. Understood?" Of course we "understood." I have the impression that even that naïve straight-A girl got it, because she suddenly went pale, sat down and didn't say another word.

In addition to our borders (which were really neither visible nor tangible, and could not be physically crossed), there were the so-called forbidden zones, areas within a radius of between about thirty and forty kilometers from the borders, which you needed a special permit from the police to visit. If you happened to be caught without one, you were automatically suspected of trying to escape. So Albania effectively had two borders: the legal boundaries between legitimate states and the forbidden zone borders, the unofficial borders of the official borders. No matter where you went, you were bound to trip up over one border or another.

This being so, the only window you got on the world-beyond-the-borders was through television and radio. We adolescents in particular were desperate to decode the messages transmitted from this alien planet, which was impossible if you didn't understand the language the aliens spoke. So, and this was especially true of the towns, a passion for foreign languages was born. Italian was the most popular.

Learning a foreign language was neither a hobby nor a luxury, nor had it any practical value; it was essential for the amazing challenge of traveling through the imagination to places that were strictly off limits, to the world-beyond-the-borders. Our imagination idealized the word-beyond-the-borders, and the more unbearably oppressive the regime at home became, the more idyllic this other world seemed to us. The regime divided the population into two strict categories: absolute good and absolute evil. We did too, but with reverse criteria: absolute evil was to be found at home and absolute good beyond our borders. Just as the regime relied on paranoid xenophobia for its continued survival, we depended on our own special brand of xenomania to resist it.

Two Years on One Border

He'll spend a few days in that shitty village where nothing ever happens, where nothing ever moves, like corpses in a graveyard, where people only know how to gossip, and to kill each other off with spite.

He'll set off on exactly the same journey—Korçë–Kalabaka, eight days on foot, because he has to make it, and so he'll cross the borders illegally ten, twelve, nineteen, thirty-six times.

The route is full of dangers. In summer there are usually soldiers guarding the footpaths who arrest anyone trying to get through illegally. There are just as many armed bandits lurking, too, waiting to pounce on and rob the illegal emigrant of what little he owns. Whoever refuses to empty his pockets gets the thrashing of his life. In winter there are fewer soldiers, fewer bandits. Instead it's a toss-up between dying in the snow or being eaten by wolves.

He still remembers that young man, just eighteen years old, burning up with fever for two days. He collapsed and died in the snow. They had to bury him and leave him. There was nothing else for it up there in the mountains. They risked getting buried in the snow themselves. They'd got caught in the most almighty snowstorm, and it was each man for himself. They trudged through it like sleepwalkers, day after day, using all their energy just to stay upright, because they knew that if they didn't, they'd be buried alive.

The one who died in the snow was called Eddy. It was his first time. They'd carried him and another lad on their backs, gasping for breath, for an entire day and night, and kept saying to him, "Be patient. We'll get there." The snow was up to their waists and he was praying to God that some military patrol would find them. But they're never there when you need them, are they?

A few hours before he died in their arms, Eddy had asked them to inform his fiancée and ask her to forgive him for not making it. They'd got engaged a couple of weeks earlier, and he'd promised that he'd come back and take her to Greece as soon as he was fixed up with a job and somewhere to live. He never got further than halfway between Korçë and Kalabaka, eight hours on foot.

He suddenly makes another calculation: thirty-four times in seven years, Albania–Greece–Albania–Greece. If you added on the days spent in detention centers each time they deported him, it was unbelievable: of the last seven years of his life, two of them have literally been spent on the borders.

8

*M*y town, Lushnjë, is close to the Adriatic. We used to spend our summer holidays by the sea. At some point the regime started putting up bunkers by the hundred thousand, the length and breadth of the country, concentrating on remote and coastal areas. We were prepared for the enemy to appear from anywhere but it seemed that the biggest menace was the enemy we waited for, and waited, and waited, and waited to invade us from the sea. The beaches we used to visit as children were suddenly filled with symbols of war. The irony was that these forbidding-looking bunkers became hot favorites for trysting lovers: temples of war rededicated to the goddess of love. Life itself was taking revenge on the paranoia of the regime.

Bunkers popped up along the beach, lying in wait for the terrible enemy, but the enemy never did us the courtesy of appearing on the horizon. In place of this terrifying enemy, the sea would wash up several humble objects from the world-beyond-the-borders: disintegrating sacks, empty Coca-Cola bottles, empty cartons of laundry detergent bearing various slogans and brand names.

People would often take these things home and decorate their houses with them. I remember a cousin of mine who was ecstatically happy when she found an empty green carton in the sea—in good condition, too. God only knows who had thrown it in from the Italian side, ignorant of the fetish status it would acquire the moment it washed up on an Albanian beach. The name of the manufacturer was printed on it, accompanied by a picture of some silky female underwear "holding hands" with its male counterpart. Both looked rather worn out after their long, difficult journey through saltwater. But my cousin was not put off; she and her mother decided that they had to take it home, and gave it pride of place in their sitting room. It could just as well have been an original Van Gogh or a Picasso.

There was something indescribably comic as well as unbearably tragic about all this. But if anyone looks beyond appearances, they might see something irreducibly human in it, too: the determination of people to cling on to the slightest contact with the world-beyond-the-borders. Just as the prisoner worships even the most trivial object from the outside because it represents freedom to him, so these people in their own tragicomic way collected evidence of the existence of a world-beyond-the-borders. It was also a way of establishing some kind of relationship with that world, a way to break through their absolute isolation and to promise themselves and others that one day all this madness would end.

The fact that the days of the regime were numbered became obvious to us when the ubiquitous statues of the Eternal Leader erected in all public squares and buildings across the country started to fall down at night. Each political system has its own sacred cows, and the sacred cows of totalitarianism are the ubiquitous public statues and portraits of Eternal Leaders, small, medium, and large: in public squares, on facades of public buildings and blocks of flats, inside public buildings, and inside people's homes. As a boy, I used to believe that statues were supposed to represent dead people. Just to make sure, I asked my mother one day, "Why are there so many statues of Uncle Enver if he's not even dead?" My mother looked at me with panic and sadness in her eyes, and said, "One day I'll tell you all about it. But don't you ever go asking your teacher questions like that." This left me with the suspicion that behind these statues lurked a terrible secret I would never be able to decipher and was not supposed to know about. Growing older, I started to understand a bit more. I realized that there was a direct analogy between the statues *and fear: as the regime intensified the fear and terror it spread among the people, the number as well as the size of the statues it put up grew proportionally.*

The tyrant's statue essentially symbolized the eternal stasis of tyranny, as the purpose of tyranny is to subject everything to a state of stasis: a stasis of thought, desire, and time itself. It aims at the predictability and stasis of the graveyard. Of course they say that when the statue of a tyrant is pulled down and tyrannical rule comes to an end, people are suddenly liberated and blossom, finding the path to truth and wealth. Sadly, this is not the case. Tyrants are merciless beasts, precisely because they leave behind distorted societies worn down by oppression and above all suffering from an orphan complex. Those who give themselves over to indiscriminate looting and destruction the minute the statues come down are like orphaned children robbing the corpse of a false and terrifying father.

After the fall of the tyrant's statue, the tortuous journey to self-knowledge begins: pieces of the statue will live on for a long time to come in the mindsets of the people who grew up and lived under tyranny.

Quiet August Days

August. The city is virtually empty. The evening newsreader makes this short announcement: "Five illegal immigrants have lost their lives, drowning at dawn off the coast of Mytilene when their boat capsized. Among them were three small children." This was the last news item before sports. The usual tragic procedure: the survivors will be put up in some kind of reception center with wretched living conditions. The usual procedure will be followed: detention, processing, deportation.

In all probability most of them will try to repeat the journey, paying dearly for it and risking life and limb in the process. Are they out of their minds? Maybe, but that's just the point. This brand of madness, this doggedness of the wanderer to enter the temple of consumerism, gambling with life itself to get there, fearing neither death nor the police, nor the dehumanizing humiliation of it all. In Morocco illegals are known as *harragas* from the Arabic verb *haraqa,* meaning "to burn." In order to avoid deportation, African illegals coming to Morocco burn their papers so that the authorities can't establish their identities. They are undocumented and therefore have no identity. They have wiped their countries off the map. Their homeland is now another country, legal or illegal. And besides, there is something that is more powerful than anything else: death has lost its sting.

9

I crossed the borders into a foreign country, Greece, on January 15, 1991. It was the first time I'd seen the borders of another country. It was the first time I'd seen the borders of my own country; the outer limits of a world that had perhaps thrown us out of time, out of the world. I thought I'd be escaping on my own, but ended up walking with an entire caravan of human beings. A caravan of human beings moving forward with one single demand: to break through that terrifying taboo otherwise known as the borders. Escape as an end in itself. Escape as illness.

I had traveled all night in a truck, hidden behind a mountain of packing cases. At one o'clock in the afternoon we reached Sarandë. We set off for the borders from somewhere round there half an hour later and arrived at around three. When they saw the human caravan making its way to the border, the driver and the codriver decided to abandon their truck and join it. We covered the final kilometers before the border post on foot. There must have been about sixty of us, mostly young men and all strangers. At the border post on the Albanian side, four soldiers holding Kalashnikovs were waiting for us with their officer, who looked at us with an expression revealing something between contempt and anger.

Officer: Where are you going?
Voice: We're leaving....

Officer: Who said that? [Silence]
Officer: Have you all got passports?
Voice: Have you given us passports?
Officer: Who said that? [Silence]
Officer: You know, things could be worse on the other side.
Voice: Let us through, let us go.
Officer: OK. Whoever wants to can go through.

We broke into a run, scared that the soldiers might shoot us in the back with their Kalashnikovs. We got through the barbed wire, which was still intact, meaning that we were the first to cross at this point. We started bashing at it with a stick to see if it was electrified and then we opened a hole in it with some sticks that the drivers had brought from their truck until it was big enough for us to get through, one at a time. In my haste, I ripped the sleeve of my coat, but at that moment my coat was the last thing on my mind. The soldiers, fingers on the triggers, looked on as we tried desperately to cut through the wire, while the officer maintained the cynical smile painted across his face.

After getting through the barbed wire we had to cross a small stream. We did so with ease, even though the water was freezing. Then we started running up a hill, looking for the first concrete signs that we had actually fled and reached the other side of the border, the other side of the world. We carried on running until someone shouted, 'We've crossed the border!' I don't know how he could tell. I can only remember hearing hysterical whoops of joy.

There were no soldiers and no policemen on the other side. We had reached the free world. We had arrived in the West. A middle-aged man threw himself to the ground, weeping, pummeling the ground rhythmically with his fists, addressing it as though it were a fellow human being. 'I've paid for you with seventeen years in prison. I've paid for you with seventeen years in prison. I've paid for you with seventeen years in prison, damn it.' Things calmed down after about half an hour until someone asked, 'Where now?' Nobody could answer him.

Everyone shrugged their shoulders in total bewilderment. We all knew where we had escaped from but not one of us knew anything about where we were going.

Some of our number spotted a dirt track and the rest of us decided to follow. A few of us could speak Greek, Greek Albanians who were immediately put in charge of our march into the unknown. As we walked, we started to speculate about what was in store for us. Someone had heard that we were going to be put up for a short while in high-rise blocks and afterward would be asked which Western country we wanted to go and work in. At that point, the two drivers of the truck jumped in, saying that they would put in a request for Germany as they were sure that there was plenty of work there, paying astronomical wages for anyone willing to make the journey from Berlin to Baghdad transporting fuel, especially now as war was about to break out in Iraq. The best news of all came from another man, who said he was sure that the road led to some harbor or other where the American fleet would be waiting for us to take us straight to the States. He almost got into a fight with another man who claimed that he had heard on Greek radio that the ships weren't American but belonged to the UN, and Albanian refugees would be taken to Italy. In the end we agreed that the ships were waiting for us, but that their provenance and destination had yet to be verified. After this, the discussion turned back to the borders. Some argued that the borders would be closed in three days' time; others said ten, while the minority opinion was that they would never close again.

In the meantime, we had come across the first houses and first residents along the road. Some Greeks had come out onto their doorsteps, and the pity on their faces was diluted only by the total astonishment they felt. The Greek speakers among us stopped to talk with them, explaining who we were and where we had come from, and asked them where we should go. Some of the old ladies offered to give us water, and that was how I learned my first words of Greek. "Efharisto," meaning "thank you" and "nero," "water," and it wouldn't be long before I added a third word to my list: "douleia"—"work."

After walking and walking we eventually arrived at our destination, a coastal village, at about eight that evening. Someone who was passing through signaled to us where we were supposed to wait for the bus that would take us to the refugee center. We all assembled there and waited. After half an hour, a man approached us, introducing himself as an Australian journalist. He wanted to know if any of us could speak English. With what little English I had managed to master I offered to talk to him. He asked us where we had crossed over from, whether the borders were guarded, where we wanted to go, what part of Albania we had come from, and what the current situation in Albania was. After getting the answers to these questions, he explained that a bus was due to arrive that would take us to a refugee center, where we would be given food, new clothes, one room between two, be taught Greek—and after a few days we would be found work. I translated all this for everyone, our future according to the Australian journalist, and they all started cheering. "This is what the West is all about!" one of the drivers called out, at the same time as urging me to ask the Australian if we would be allowed to go and work in a country of our choice. I didn't get the chance to ask either about that or about the ships waiting for us at the unspecified harbor to take us to America, Italy, or wherever else our starved imaginations desired. The Australian had vanished, leaving us alone with our fantasies.

A few started allocating the bedrooms we were supposed to be sharing. The two drivers unsurprisingly decided in an instant that they would share. For others it was harder to find a roommate, so the drivers, relieved of that particular anxiety, volunteered to sort everyone out. First we counted the number of couples. None of them were married; this was a problem. We had no idea whether the regulations permitted unmarried couples to stay together, and besides, we didn't even know if men and women would be housed together or in separate quarters.

We came up with a temporary solution while we waited for the bus that was to take us to what we all had started calling the refugee center. Some of the group, mainly the younger boys, went and pressed their faces up against the window of a nearby café. They were gawking in astonishment at the color television and the images it transmitted. The patrons of the café gawked back at the Albanians gawking in astonishment at their color television with a corresponding degree of astonishment. Eventually someone got up and came to the door. He was holding a biscuit tin and started throwing biscuits at us, in the way that you would toss grain to pigeons, or corn to chickens or ducks. Some of us tried to catch the biscuits. And that was when I was reminded that I had a stomach attached to my body and realized that I was hungry.

Some of our group just stood there, glued to the TV screen through the café window. One of them, he must have been about twenty, his face badly worn by the sun and exhaustion, suddenly swung round and whispered in an innocent, stunned tone, "But there's no sex!" Perhaps he'd imagined that in the world-beyond-the-borders, just as my old high school friend had claimed, there is a constant ambush of sex and as soon as darkness falls, something along the lines of an all-night orgy begins. This was also part of the fantasy that we had carried with us.

The Gender of Borders

We don't all cross in the same way. The authority of the borders reminds us all of our very different origins, different classes, different castes, different skin color, and, above all, different genders.

March 18. She left that day. She was only seventeen. Everybody was getting out. The country was like a poisoned organism that purged itself of people in its effort to survive. But none of the girls had left town, not until then, at least. She was the first.

People were rushing to get out of hell while there was still time. They say that hell is one place, but in reality, hell is private and particular to each one of us. She wanted to escape hers: her father. For as long as she could remember she had wanted to leave, to escape. Escape his shouting, his hateful looks, her mother's screeching, which she still heard in her sleep. She stills shivers today when she recalls that threatening knock on the door. As soon as she heard it, she knew exactly what was going to happen. The same routine over and over again, the same methods. Music; he would always turn the volume up on the radio to smother her screams. That was the only time music was heard in their house. He would pummel her head with his fists like a madman until his hands were sore. Then he'd remove his belt, and whip her entire body with it, until the point where her skin split open and her flesh bled, the same words punctuating the thrashings: "You ought to be ashamed of yourself!"

Human beings have an incredibly high pain threshold and can suffer abject humiliation and degradation if they are convinced that there's no way out. I can't say whether they accept it or just get used to it, but they do learn to live with it, thinking there is no alternative. That was true of this girl; she had just about come to terms with the fact that this is what her life was like and always would be like. I say just about because there was something that was helping her to keep it together, and that was her dream of becoming an actress. That's what she wanted more than anything. Perhaps it was because for as long as she could remember, she had wanted to live the lives of other people and not her own.

She was in the last year of high school. There was a theater group at school she went along to, behind his back. But he found out about it one day and the curtain went up on the same old show: music, punches, belt, screaming, blood, but a different script this time: "Actress? Over my dead body!"

A week later she heard that they'd opened the borders. At first not that many people were leaving, but gradually more and more decided to go. All the men left. She wanted to leave, too. She could think about nothing else. She had to leave. But how—and who with?

She'd never seen him before. The first time she saw him was when her cousin introduced them. It was raining heavily and she found it hard to see his features clearly. But her desire to leave was so overwhelming that it blurred her vision. "I came back from Greece three days ago, and I'm off again the day after tomorrow," he told her. "I'm told that you want to leave—I can get you to Athens and help you find work."

"Yes. I do want to leave. If you can take me to Athens, I'll pay you back as soon I get a job."

"That's easy enough," he answered. "See you the day after tomorrow."

They arranged to meet a short distance outside town. Lying awake all night, she got up in the morning, took her school bag, replacing her books with a few clothes, some childhood photos, a few slices of bread, and some olives for the journey. She opened the front door slowly. He had left early, as usual, and gone to work. So had her mother. She stepped out onto the street, stopping occasionally to look back because she had the feeling that he was secretly following her, that he'd suddenly jump out in front of her, just like ghosts do in children's nightmares.

She arrived on time. Her cousin's contact appeared shortly afterward. She had barely greeted him when a truck pulled up in front of her. "Jump in," he told her, "before they see us." She jumped in and recognized the face of her cousin at the back, surprised to see him, as he hadn't told her that he was planning on coming along. He was very cool toward her and the only thing he said was, "It was a last-minute thing." The truck started. That was important to her. She kept saying to herself, "I'm not dreaming, I'm leaving. I'm actually leaving!" They slowly left the villages behind them, the towns, and the people of Albania, but, most importantly, him: her father.

About halfway there, sometime in the afternoon, they stopped to eat. Everybody got out of the truck. She was the only girl. She counted the men. Seven. She couldn't eat a thing. She was so anxious her stomach tied itself up in knots. When they finished their food, that character pulled her to one side and said, in a menacing voice, "You're looking a little thoughtful. If you're having second thoughts, forget it. There's no turning back now."

Everyone got back into the truck to continue the journey to the borders. Most of the time nobody said a word. He was sitting close to her now, every now and then "accidentally" resting his hand on her leg, her breast, her shoulders. She went numb. Only at that moment did she ask herself, "Who is this man? Who am I with?"

She searched out her cousin's face in a desperate plea for help, but he wasn't even looking in her direction any longer. She could cry for help, but to whom? She started shaking with fear. In her desperation to escape her father's authority she had failed to appreciate that her father was just another link in a chain of violence that had been simmering below the surface for so many years and was waiting to erupt like a volcano.

Two days later they reached the area outside Gjirokastër.[3] The truck stopped. It was dark. The driver announced that they'd be spending the night there: The border was only a couple of hours away on foot, but it was best to cross at dawn. "You have to cross when they're between shifts because there aren't any guards about then." She got out of her seat and climbed down out of the truck. "Where do you think you're going?" he asked her threateningly. "I need to stretch my legs," she answered. It was pitch black outside and you could hardly see anything at all. But after a while her vision adjusted to the darkness and she could make out a few houses in a small village in the distance. She started walking, carefully moving away from the truck. She got quite far. She turned back to make sure no one had seen her. She stopped and stared at those small village houses. Everyone would be asleep at this time of night, but what if she tried to run there to ask for help? How long would she need? Ten, fifteen minutes? Of course they'd open up, if they saw a young girl alone begging for help.

Just at that moment she was grabbed violently by the hair and pulled to the ground. "Whore! Doing a runner, were we, scum?" He grabbed her hair again and pushed her face into the ground. She couldn't breathe. "Who exactly do you think you are? Coming across all innocent when you're nothing but an old whore. If you weren't, you wouldn't have left with me, would you?" With a sudden violent jerk, he turned her over and ripped open her sweater. She started screaming at the top of her lungs, crying for help and lashing at him with all her strength. But she was no match for him, using one hand to punch her and the other to cover her mouth. She couldn't breathe, but still tried to hit him wherever she could. His hand was stuck to her face like some phenomenally strong suction cup until very gradually her breath failed her.

They say that a short while before you die your entire life flashes in front of you. That's what happened to her. She relived all her life, everything she had left behind: her mother's face, old before its time, her eyes (she'd never been able to understand why they weren't permanently full of tears); her father's screams; the threatening knock on the door; the music; the belt; the punches; the screaming; the blood; prison; hell; the words after every beating, "You ought to be ashamed of yourself." "Actress? Over my dead body."

She stopped hitting him. She could feel his filthy breath on her and she dug her nails deep into the earth. At that moment her soul left her body, leaving him with the empty shell. I don't know how long it took because, for her, time had come to a standstill, but she collected together whatever remnants of her soul she could find and re-entered the hollow shell. Blood was flowing down her legs. She staggered to her feet, walking in a daze. She could hear his voice calling after her in the dark, mocking her. "Look! She liked it so much, she's drunk on it!" Other voices joining in. She struggled a few steps further until she could hear her cousin gloating, "That's what happens to all of them, all the ones who fancy themselves as artists. Still like the theater, do you?" She looked like a robot. She pulled herself up into the truck, curled up in a corner like a wounded animal, and slept the deepest sleep of her life.

She was woken at dawn by voices telling her to get up. They were starting off for the border. Trekking through bushes, her clothes kept snagging on thorns and her jacket got ripped. Suddenly they came to a stream and her shoes got soaked, so she had to continue barefoot. After trudging along for quite some time, they were nearing the Albanian border post. It looked abandoned; no one there. Someone gave the order to run because Albanian soldiers often deliberately kept out of sight. They all started running at once. The soles of her feet were bleeding but she still tried to run as fast as she could. Three gunshots were fired and she felt something burning on her. Her hair had caught fire. She threw herself to the ground and somehow managed to beat out the flames with her hands. The bullets had just skimmed the surface of her skull. She was on her feet again, her knees bloodied, her hands burnt and very painful, but she went on. Nothing could stop her. She had already crossed the border. Back there at Gjirokastër.

10

The bus did eventually turn up and take us to the so-called refugee center, where all the other Albanian fugitives who'd arrived before us were assembled. Only the bus wasn't a bus but a filthy truck. We climbed in. It was already very dark and I can't remember exactly how long the journey took, only that we were all squeezed in tight next to each other and hardly said a word. We'd suddenly run out of enthusiasm and it was only then, after all those hours, that we started to feel anxious about the unknown.

The truck came to a standstill and we realized we were supposed to get out. When we did we saw Greek policemen shouting and brandishing their truncheons in an effort to impose order. A single spotlight illuminated the scene: Greek soldiers and an enormous crowd of Albanian fugitives. From the policemen's gestures, we gathered that they wanted us to stand in a line. We formed a huge line, new arrivals, all of whom had to be registered: name, surname, father's name. I saw the two drivers looking rather nervously at the policemen who were pacing up and down, brandishing their truncheons and bellowing at us. They looked as though they were asking themselves why angry policemen had to carry truncheons in the West as well.

After waiting for about an hour in the line, it was our turn. We stood in front of a table while a policeman asked us, one after the other, in rhythmic, broken Albanian: "Ermi? Biemri? Ermi babai?"—*Name?*

Surname? Father's name? I smiled at his efforts. He responded with a look that seemed to say, "That's the last thing you want to be doing now, you poor idiot!" I handed him my Albanian identity card, he took down my details, and I stepped aside, waiting for Xhemal to finish. I had met Xhemal on the escape journey. When the policeman asked to see his identity card, Xhemal answered with a phrase that does not exist in any language on earth: "pashaport kaput," which was amplified by a hand gesture indicating decapitation, as though it was his identity card that had had its head severed. The policeman stared at him, as though he had just sighted a UFO, until it dawned on him what Xhemal was trying to say. When he did, he returned to the formula: "Ermi? Biemri? Ermi babai?" But even in this Xhemal's originality shone through: apparently his name was Dhimitris Dhimas, son of Vasilis Dhimas.

When he finished I asked him what that was all in aid of, and he told me that Greeks look on Christian names in a more positive light than Muslim ones: Muslim names scare them. One of the drivers quickly jumped in, reprimanding Xhemal for his lie. "This is the West, this is a democracy, all men are equal. And since when were we Albanians religious, anyway?" he added in the tones of a schoolteacher. The truth is that over the next few days it was hard to judge what precise advantage the name Dimitris yielded Xhemal. He was staying with us, in the same place, in what looked like a warehouse, behind the village soccer field. During the registration process, we discovered that the name of the village was Filiates.

You Weren't Invited

Illegal immigrant. That's your nickname. That's your name. That's your label. After all, you turned up here without an invitation. That's how people used to migrate in the days before World War I, uninvited, without visas. But that was a very long time ago and things are different now. And if you think that by reminding the locals of that time, they'll start feeling sorry for you and accept you, you're living in cloud cuckoo land. You won't just be an illegal immigrant if you go around doing that, you'll be an impudent illegal immigrant.

The fact that you arrived uninvited makes you feel uncomfortable, and deeply guilty, and you may never get over that feeling. Because apart from everything else, they keep reminding you of the fact. This is your original sin. Each time you try to stand up for yourself, you'll hear it: nobody asked you to come. Each time you try to break out of this obscurity, they'll be there to remind you that you're an unwanted guest.

You tell them that you want to be legalized, that it's unbearable trembling every time you see a Black Maria and, anyway, who wants to feel like a scared mouse all the time because he hasn't got the right papers in his pocket? I may have arrived without an invitation but I work just like the rest of you do, I pay the same taxes as the rest of you do, and most importantly, my boss, or rather, my bosses, need me. Yes, I do realize that you are feeding me, but let me tell you that I more than repay it. Yes, I am dependent on you for my survival, but you depend on me for your wealth. That's life. Give and take. I have started to build a new life here, I have got used to this city, and who knows, this city might eventually get used to me. So why am I illegal and worse than a stray dog? The city is deaf to your defense. The city is deaf. And on the news, the journalists give voice to the vox pop and want to make sure that you never manage to shake off your nickname, your name, your label: illegal immigrant, illegal life, illegal.

11

*A*fter registration we were told to go to the churchyard, where we would be given something to eat. We ate in the same way all hungry people the world over eat. Meanwhile, Albanian fugitives continued to pour into the so-called refugee center, seemingly endlessly. It was as though the entire country had made a unanimous decision to take advantage of the open borders and get out as quickly as possible. The policemen and soldiers looked on in astonishment at the unending human caravan and found it hard to comprehend. "If this goes on much longer, there won't be anything left in Albania apart from the trees," said Xhemal.

Since we'd managed to satisfy our hunger a bit with a helping of spaghetti, we started discussing how long we thought it would take for Albania to catch up with Greece. One of the drivers reckoned about five years. The other thought more like fifteen, while Xhemal, who'd been temporarily overcome by some sort of melancholy, had the last word: "It'll never happen; Albania can't move forward as long as Albanians are running it." Later, after our hunger had abated, we started to feel the cold. It was freezing and it was then that we understood that before we could work out how many years it would take for Albania to catch up with Greece, we'd have to decide what was going to become of us that night.

The big warehouse where they put us up was full. The few foam mattresses they'd laid out had already been taken over by weary bodies, *which had been walking for hours if not days. Whoever found an empty corner of unoccupied foam to lay his head on was very lucky. We slowly realized that the high-rise block of flats, with one room for two people, hot running water, and new clothes that the Australian journalist had promised us might be a long time coming.*

The Strange Habits of Illegal Immigrants

Those who cross borders illegally develop strange habits. Laughing too much is one of them. They are overcome by a mood for fun and jokes, as though they have just emerged from some side-splitting revue when in fact danger and the threat of death is all around them. Perhaps it's the imminence of death and the fear of it that provoke this laughter. It's as though they want to cajole and seduce death. Human laughter is the perfect cover, it's like telling death, "There's no way you're getting us. Look at us—we're laughing, we're not even thinking about you. We love life. We want to live. We want to survive. You'll have to look elsewhere for customers. You won't find any here."

12

I spent the night on the legs of one of my compatriots, and when I woke in the morning, I found another compatriot asleep on my own. I was forced to wake him so that I could get up. Xhemal was already awake. So were the two drivers. They beckoned me over to join them. We had already formed a solid friendship, despite meeting only yesterday. The drivers from Tiranë, Xhemal from Elbasan, and myself, from Lushnjë. That's the way people make friends and form groups when they're far from home and miserable. Unpredictable alliances, just like teenagers. The police allowed us to move around freely and go wherever we pleased. The young lad from the previous night who had asked why there wasn't any sex on the color TV in the café joined us, too. He never said a word and had the look of someone who was searching for something he knew was somewhere close by, but still couldn't find. After the episode outside the coffee shop, we all called him Sex Boy.

We left the warehouse and went for a short stroll round the village and ended up in a café. The drivers had ten dollar coins with them, which to us seemed like a small fortune. They were going to treat us to coffee or tea. To my good fortune, the owner of the café could speak Italian, so I was able to help the drivers change some of their dollars into drachmas. The proprietor took the dollars and examined them closely, first in natural and then artificial light. After satisfying himself that there was nothing suspect about the money, he went ahead with *the exchange, and we looked on with almost religious piety. The drivers took the drachmas, most of it in notes, and then gave the rest of us permission to look at them. Xhemal made the first comment. "There you go. Normal stuff. Not like ours, all full of pictures of soldiers and hammer drills."*

At some point the proprietor spoke to us again, telling me that he'd once been an immigrant in Italy and Germany but had come home a few years ago and opened the café. "What did you come here for?" he asked me. I felt a bit uncomfortable. What should I say? That we wanted to cross the border to avoid spending the rest of our lives going insane in a despicable prison? Instead I told him that we were hoping for a better life and to live like the rest of the world did. He listened while he dried a glass on a tea towel, and in the end let a cynical smirk cross his face. "Poor bastards. You've no idea what you've let yourselves in for," and the cynical smirk was slowly replaced by an enigmatic expression, as if he'd just delivered the most profound prophecy in history. "What do you mean?" I asked him, trying to understand the first messages from this new planet we had just landed on. The two drivers, Xhemal and Sex Boy, were desperately trying to follow this conversation. The owner eventually resumed his normal expression and started saying that the fate of an immigrant is always really shit, and when you arrive somewhere uninvited, then it's a million times more shit. "Even the worst country in the world is better than a foreign country," he concluded, lit a cigarette and took a sharp intake of breath, as though he wanted to expel something that had lodged itself in his throat.

Because I couldn't stand the pressure of my companions, who wanted instant translations of everything, I just told them what I had understood. At first they went all quiet, trying to decipher the meaning of the conversation, and then one of the drivers tried to give his interpretation: "He wants to sell us something. It's all got to do with these Greeks and their Trojan horses." The rest said nothing, at a loss as to what the connection between an ex-immigrant Greek café owner, the shitty fate of immigrants, and the Trojan horse might be.

The Supermarket Door

Each time he makes the journey from Korçë to Kalabaka, eight days on foot, the illegal immigrant tells a lot of jokes. He always tells the story about the supermarket, which never fails to get even the most morose members of the group laughing.

It was the first time he'd been to a supermarket. Back home there weren't any. At first he'd lived on diet of souvlaki, two solid months of souvlaki, until he was sick of the sight of it. One evening, when he'd just knocked off work and got his first wages, he decided to go to the supermarket. He got to the entrance, and saw that the door kept opening and closing as people went in and out. But when he tried to go inside, it refused to open. He tried once more, and again. Nothing. He took ten paces back and watched to see how other people were managing to get in. Everybody else seemed to be getting in without any difficulty. He tried again, this time moving more quickly. Nothing. He tried a slower approach; nothing. He'd turned red with embarrassment and frustration. Then he spotted a gentleman reversing through the doors. Interesting. He tried that, too, turning his back to the door. Nothing. He was at a loss. How come all these people were entering and leaving the supermarket so effortlessly, while he, no matter what he tried, failed? Perhaps the door had a thing about Albanians. That might be it. So he tried to do the most obvious thing, trail one of the other customers as they went in. Why hadn't he thought of that earlier, idiot? But at that moment nobody seemed to be going in. "Just my bloody luck," he whispered. Then he saw his salvation; an extremely obese woman, waddling along like a wounded duck, who stood no chance of getting into the supermarket unless both doors opened. He started following her, trying to look casual, from behind, in what was perhaps his last hope of getting in; he was determined not to waste this chance, but in his anxiety he got a bit too close to her, with the result that when he saw the door open, he all but pushed her inside. Realizing that he'd finally crossed the threshold of the supermarket, he apologized to the lady. He was sweating as though he had just finished the 200-meter hurdles. The woman shot him a dirty look, borderline homicidal, and he, embarrassed, quickly moved away to the sound of her muttering. He couldn't be sure but he thought he could make out the word "Albanian."

The others were listening, laughing, laughing again, some louder than others, the ones making the eight-day journey from Korçë to Kalabaka on foot for the first time. But at that moment someone started shouting, in a strained voice, the voice a hunter uses when he finally tracks down the quarry he's been after for days. "Quiet. Everyone down. Border patrol." Everyone fell silent and dropped to the ground, flush with the earth. One with the earth.

13

*A*fter a few minutes' silence I found the courage to ask the café owner if he could find me a book that would help me learn Greek. He pointed outside through the window and told me I could get them from a bookshop, as those sorts of books were very cheap. Of course I didn't continue the conversation, as I wasn't in a position to buy so much as a stone from the street, let alone an entire book. I asked him if he could give me a job, so I could earn some money and buy some books and learn some Greek. He said he'd think about it and let me know. We sipped our coffee, watching images from the war in Iraq on the TV. They had absolutely no effect on us, though. We had our own battle to fight.

Just as we were getting up to leave, a scream was heard, a scream so loud that it made my hair stand on end. It was the owner. He looked ready to kill. I was terrified by this transformation and the only reason for this metamorphosis that I could think of was that he'd discovered that the drivers' dollars were counterfeit. He came rushing over to us, grabbed Sex Boy by the arm, and pulled him off in the direction of the toilets. Sex Boy didn't resist at all. I was completely bewildered. So was everyone else. The owner and Sex Boy disappeared behind the whole door marked "Toilette" while we sat there exchanging looks in silence. A minute later the white door opened again and the owner and Sex Boy emerged. The *owner seemed a little calmer, and made a gesture as if to say, "OK, you can all go back to where you came from now."*

Once outside we asked Sex Boy what the hell was going on. "I pissed and missed," he answered, with the naturalness of someone who had just been asked their name. To cut a long story short, some of his urine had splashed onto the toilet seat. "So what happened?" we asked him. "Nothing. He told me to clean it and I did," he replied in the same matter-of-fact way. "And that's why he was behaving as though we'd killed his mother?" asked one of the drivers. "Bloody Greek," added the other driver, the one who'd earlier volunteered the theory about the Trojan horse and who at that moment was vowing to boycott the café and told the rest of us that we should, too. Then Xhemal spoke: "We Albanians don't even know how to piss any more. Fucking communism." And, with that, he brought the conversation to a close.

Work, Work, Work

Being an immigrant can mean a lot of things, but most of all it means work. You don't emigrate so you can play the tough guy, but to save up money. You will do anything to succeed in this: you take on two, maybe three jobs a day, without insurance, of course, undercutting the going rate for the locals; you become a strike breaker, and if need be, you try selling sob stories to your employers to get their sympathy until you realize that sympathy is in short supply; you turn up in Omonia Square at dawn on the off-chance that there's some work available, and you stand there waiting like some filthy municipal statue nobody can be bothered to clean; you live in a cave, with another ten, fifteen, maybe twenty people, blurring the distinction between home and pigsty; you eat bread and salt, or just bread; you always doze off on the bus from exhaustion and lack of sleep; your stale sweat can be smelled a mile off, because you don't have time to wash and you need to economize on electricity. You make even the most tight-fisted look generous. You count out your money with the same precision as the anemic monitors drops of blood during a transfusion. You spend nothing, you buy nothing, you live on only the absolute necessities—only counting money satisfies you, that and the thought of more work, even more work. Suddenly, without warning, your strength starts to fail you, arthritis strikes, you get suspect pains in your kidneys, your back, and your heart. You'll be lucky if you make it into the operating theater. Many don't. They die on the job; some wall or other collapses on top of them, because their bosses don't want the expense of making the site safe. Because everyone knows that immigrants die silently, like flies.

14

We went to get the bus to the big town. They told us we might find work in Igoumenitsa. While we waited at the bus stop some passers-by had directed us to, we started talking about cars. Xhemal thought that the price of a car was the equivalent of about ten days' work. The drivers thought about a month. Sex Boy and I said nothing. Xhemal and the drivers went on tirelessly and after a while got into the different makes they were going to drive. Xhemal preferred French manufacturers, the drivers German. And that was when we all found out that cars were Xhemal's great love.

He used to drive a car himself, and was more familiar with their design than he was with the insides of his own pockets, as he put it. "I only worked as a driver for one year. I drove a municipal shitmobile, and in the end they took that away from me, too."

Standing there in the cold, waiting for the bus, Xhemal started to tell us all about his relationship with the shitmobile, or the yellow car, as he sometimes referred to it on account of its color. The shitmobile was a special municipal vehicle that had something to do with the sewage system. When Xhemal finished his military service, driving the shitmobile was the best job he could get. He found it humiliating at the time, because he felt he was destined for higher things, but need prevailed. Oddly enough, it was while driving the shitmobile that he experienced the best and the worst days of his life. Xhemal narrated with great passion and a touch *of theatricality, as though he had been waiting for this moment for years, there at the stop, waiting for the bus that would take us to Igoumenitsa, to pour out his heart. It was all about a girl, who just happened to be one of the most beautiful in town.*

The Kitchen Dogsbody Generation

The first generation of immigrants is the kitchen dogsbody generation. These immigrants get the worst of it: the negativity, the contempt, the fear. To them, all jobs are good jobs, as long as they get their stomachs filled with a little leftover. That little leftover is the reward, their therapy, the Promised Land, the big lie, the promise of return. This is the generation that can't get the language right, or doesn't speak at all, the generation that is terrified of the police, who live in fear of their boss's look, who consume loneliness in silence, who bend right down as far as the dust, who store up as much money as resentment. Resentment is their fortress, it is where their fear resides, the negativity of the locals, the contempt, the pressure and the ridicule of employers. This is the kitchen dogsbody generation. This generation does not have furniture at home, not unless it's been chucked onto the trash heap by some local who has replaced it with something new. For the kitchen dogsbody generation there is no such thing as a holiday. There is only one thing: work. The dream of going home embracing the dream of staying on because that's just it; the kitchen dogsbody generation is schizophrenic at heart.

15

Xhemal hadn't even been driving his shitmobile for two weeks when he first met Alba at a cousin's house. It was love at first sight for both of them, something straight out of a romantic novel. She was in the last year of high school and, being the daughter of a high-ranking army officer, was able to avoid school without any difficulty. She would often get excused from lessons on spurious grounds, and the teachers never minded. Xhemal, on the other hand, would take the day off, usually without making excuses. They would meet on the outskirts of town and drive to the fields outside town in the shitmobile. They often made love in it, too.

One day, the sewer in the Party Central Committee building got blocked, and unfortunately for Xhemal, they were expecting a very distinguished visitor to arrive from Tirana that day. They quickly tried to alert him and his shitmobile, but neither vehicle nor driver were anywhere to be found. When he later got back to work, he walked into a state of war, and it was a miracle that they didn't take away his car then and there. He got off with a horrible reprimand and a warning.

Less than a week later disaster struck the happy lovers. Alba's father committed suicide. One morning, just like any other, he walked out onto his balcony holding a pistol to his temples, screaming, "I am no traitor. Long live the Party! Long live our glorious army!" and pulled the trigger. It was a terrible sight, because Alba's house was right in the center of town, and at that hour everyone was on their way to work. Some said that her father's brains landed a whole kilometer away from their block of flats. But perhaps these calculations can be put down to the usual tendency of the townspeople to exaggeration.

At first they said that Alba's father had lost his mind. Later it was discovered that he'd been accused of being a traitor. No one could say what or whom he had betrayed. The official line was the last word from Party Central Committee. They said that he was a member of a group of conspirators inside the army preparing the ground for a foreign invasion of Albania. Opinions were divided on the subject of the ring of conspirators. Some said they were Russian agents; others thought they were American. There was a third version, which had them down as Russian-American double agents. The fourth interpretation was one that terrified everybody. People were used to groups of conspirators periodically coming to light, either in the army, from among teachers or agricultural cooperatives, even from within the ranks of the Party, and sometimes completely random individuals, and such revelations were followed with persecution and imprisonment. That was when people started to be afraid of their own shadows, because any one of them was a potential traitor.

Drowning Your Sorrows in Adult Cinemas

He imagined that this city would resemble one enormous supermarket where he could get anything he wanted: dreams, happiness, prosperity, even love. That's what it looked like from a distance, anyway, but now, standing in the center, he's feeling dizzy and scared. Because everything around him looks so cold, so fast, so soulless, so indifferent.

In this city he is suffering from appalling loneliness, so much so that he even envies the stray dogs. He's young: nice things excite him a lot, especially nice-looking girls. At night, when he goes to sleep, he runs his hands across his body in a caress, to stem the hunger of his famished flesh, his loneliness.

Late on Saturday night, when he gets off work, despite his exhaustion, he takes the bus downtown and goes into an adult cinema. It's his only entertainment, the only thing that gets his adrenalin going, his only outlet, the only thing he doesn't count the cost of. He later emerges onto the street full of self-loathing and the loneliness comes back in a crueler form. He walks toward the red-light district, to Metaxourgeio, where he remembered seeing a brothel with a sign outside written in Albanian: GREEKS ONLY.

The following week, on Saturday night, he will go back to the same cinema. He will walk out onto the pavement after the show, once more full of self-loathing, and his loneliness will intensify and become even crueler. He'll go walking around the red-light district again, and read the same sign in Albanian: Greeks only.

One day he saw a cousin of his in one of the city's brothels. She was very pale; she looked like a naked ghost. He cried a lot that night without really knowing why: his country, his loneliness, his cousin? Perhaps all three.

16

After the Commandant's suicide, Alba and her mother were exiled for a month. She didn't appear at all during that time, didn't go to school, just sat shut up at home all day. Every day Xhemal would wait outside her school in the shitmobile with the hope that at some point she would come walking out. And then he found out that she'd been exiled. One of the laborers working with him told him. He lived across the road from her. He told Xhemal that a Jeep had turned up, one of those military police ones, accompanied by about a dozen policemen, in the middle of the night. Alba's hair-raising screams had pierced the darkness. "Don't exile us. We're innocent." Nobody dared go to their windows, everyone just stood watching from behind their curtains. So did he, his eyes round with fear. He told Xhemal that they weren't even given time to pack, but he did see Alba carrying a suitcase. "Even though it was dark, I could make out her face. Ashen white, like a corpse."

That day Xhemal drank a lot. So much that driving the famous shitmobile around the town center, he lost control and went crashing into a shop front. Thankfully by then it was the middle of the night and the shop was closed, otherwise there would have been bloodshed. The window was shattered, and he escaped with nothing more than a broken arm. But that wasn't the worst of it. Unluckily for him, stretched across the façade of the building was a gigantic poster of our Great Leader, bearing in enormous letters the caption: "May you live like the high mountains, comrade Enver." It had been there since the Great Leader's birthday celebrations. For that reason, even though he was bent double in agony, he was held for questioning at the station. Fortunately he passed out, so they had no choice but to transfer him to hospital. God knows what would have happened to him if they hadn't.

His troubles were not quite over, however. When he was discharged from hospital, he was sent for questioning at an emergency Party meeting where he first heard innuendos about relationships with enemies of the Party, obvious references to Alba. He was lucky in this, too: his father, an old communist, knew some people who managed to get him off with a sacking.

"What about Alba? Did you see her again?" asked Sex Boy. Xhemal looked down. He took a deep breath and said, "They found her body a month later. She'd slashed her wrists." A profound silence engulfed us, one that nobody dared disturb.

First Words

The immigrant is a creature surrounded by borders. Conventional borders, the ones that divide one country from another, mean little to him, they are just large, visible borders. There are thousands of invisible borders, however, awaiting him every minute of every day, awaiting his every move, almost, his every desire and ambition. The language: behold the first invisible border. What immigrant has not lived through the initial bewilderment—something resembling first love— that you feel when you pronounce your first sentences in a foreign language, which until the previous day had sounded like hammer blows to you, or like a sewing machine running up a hem? You try to import unusual phrases and expressions into your speech, especially the ones you think will bridge the gulf between you and the native speakers: *re paidi mou* (look, kid); *oxi re gamoto* (oh, fuck); *einai moufa* (crap); *mou ti dineis* (you get on my nerves); *Christos kai Panagia* (Jesus and mother of God), as well as the ubiquitous *malaka* (asshole). All of this you try to say in as convincing an accent as you can, hoping to pass for a native, as far as possible, and convince them that you can become one of them.

17

I had gone numb. Not from hearing the story about the shitmobile and the suicide of beautiful, tragic Alba, as I couldn't be sure how much truth there was in it and how much was a product of Xhemal's imagination. It was strange, but just as the company immigrants keep is unpredictable, the individuals it is made up of are equally unpredictable. Your flight gives you incredible freedom: suddenly you feel the need to spill the innermost secrets of your heart to complete strangers with an ease that might be seen as mad or just base. Maybe all this happens because when you leave, you also leave behind the weight of commitments. For that reason, you're not really telling your story: it's more an exercise in confession. Whatever the case, real or invented, Alba's story was a terrible one, but by the standards of our towns and cities, not that unusual. I was numb mostly because I felt that something significant had taken place in my life. I had crossed the borders. Was that not one of my biggest dreams? Yes, it was. But I could not, how can I put it—take off. From within the madness of totalitarianism, I had imagined that as soon as I crossed the borders, a completely different life would start, a whole new world. And it was. The world I saw around me was completely different. At least very different from the one I'd been living in until yesterday. I was free in the world-beyond-the-borders. A strange feeling had taken over me, one I couldn't describe. I felt like an orphaned child—completely free but at the same time completely lost. I looked at the road signs and tried to make sense of those *incomprehensible letters. "I will never be able to learn this language," said one of the drivers. "Why don't those Greeks write like everybody else?"* added Xhemal, *convinced that the rest of the planet was committed to the Latin alphabet. Meanwhile, the drivers had fixed their gaze on a church near the bus stop we'd been standing at for so long. "Doesn't that look like a mosque?" commented one of them, with the confidence of a specialist on Byzantine and Ottoman places of worship. Then, for the first time, Sex Boy revealed his knowledge: "Those are mosques that were converted into churches when they kicked the Turks out of Greece."*

One more source of confusion had thus been cleared up, this time of a divine rather than a secular nature. The bus eventually appeared and we boarded it. The conductor asked to see our tickets. The drivers decided to handle this. "Albania fukara; Albania refugiat," which loosely translates from this improvised language as "We are poor Albanian refugees." The conductor was angry. Who knows how many Albanians had been using the same line on his buses recently. I understood enough to know that he was warning us that if he caught us again without a ticket, he'd kick us off.

We were bunched together at the back of the bus, and all the other passengers had turned round to listen to our exchange with the conductor, which probably looked more like a conversation between the deaf than anything else. I went up to one of the drivers and whispered in his ear that he really should buy us some tickets with the money he'd changed back at the café because we were making a bad impression on the other passengers. He turned, gave me a filthy look, and after a short pause said, "I didn't realize you were such an asshole." The others seemed to agree. The episode was soon forgotten because, in the last analysis, we were happy to be on our way to a big town, a thoroughbred capitalist town, as Xhemal put it.

Remember, Foreigner

The more competent you become at the language, the more likely you think you are to make it. *That's it*, you say to yourself, full of excitement. The natives start asking you how you managed to learn so fast, and you feel their eyes on you, maybe for the first time looking at you with admiration. Or did you just imagine it? You start to believe that the road into their world is now open; even your boss speaks to you differently. It's just that at the end of the week, when it's payday, he remembers that you're a foreigner. And the distance asserts itself again.

And as the days go by, the weeks, the months, you realize that speaking the language is not enough. They never miss the chance to remind you that you are foreign: on the news; at the Aliens' Bureau; when you try to rent a flat and read that sign on the door saying, "No foreigners. No pets." And if the color of your skin is different then you have another reason to remember that you are a foreigner, mostly from the curses you hear and the looks you get. The look a white man gives a black man is not hard to decipher.

You're reminded at work when your boss pays you. You're reminded on the street, during the operations sweep and the identity spot checks. You're reminded on the bus, when the natives shout: "These foreigners take up our seats," or when they warn each other, "Keep an eye on your wallet— bloody light-fingered Albanians." You're reminded at the bar, when the local girls find out where you're from and vanish. And so on and so on, over and over again.

18

*When we arrived in Igoumenitsa we got the shock of our lives.
The cafés were full of people, especially young people. The
shops were bright, and still decorated with Christmas lights.
Advertisements everywhere. Expensive cars and expensive clothes. All
five of us looked on in bewilderment. Without giving it much thought, we
decided that this was the perfect place to find work and live. "You see, you
idiots, what we've been missing because of communism?" asked Xhemal
in a tone that suggested that he was talking more to himself than to us.
We didn't know where to look and then one of the drivers, who had a
bent for theoretical discussion, said the words that ignited yet another
heated debate in the biting cold: "The Greeks are lucky. They always
have been. Ever since ancient times." And he went on, and an entire
reservoir of historical knowledge flooded out, explaining to us how Greece
had only escaped communism by the skin of its teeth, thanks to the
Americans, and that the Greeks were now living off the fat of Europe
and that basically they did nothing except go to the beach in the summer
and stay out late having fun. "Why didn't they get Hoxha instead of us?
Bastards," he wondered, putting a full stop to his historical marathon.
It was just that he addressed this last question to the heavens, as though
in communion with a superior being or expecting some kind of concrete
answer from God Himself. Then Xhemal, who always entered into these
discussions with plenty of zeal, answered, "Because we're a bunch of*

assholes. That's why." Instead of the skies, Xhemal looked at the driver with the look of a gladiator before a fight. He didn't react, neither did the other driver. Neither did I. Only Sex Boy found the courage to speak up. He said something vague about fate, and that history is nothing but a lousy old whore. It seemed that we'd covered everything in our oral interpretation of history, so we went on.

Walking around the town we saw a few building sites. We'd all learned the Greek word for work, "douleia," the night before. Sex Boy and I approached some workmen and tried it out: "Douleia?" I said. "No douleia," came the answer from one of them, who seemed to me to be smiling with pity. We abandoned the idea and tried another site. "Douleia?" Instead of an answer we received an entire cascade of what was to us meaningless language. Judging by the expression on the man's face, we understood that he was angry with us for speaking to him and were to get out of his sight as quickly as possible.

That's what we did. While we were walking, Sex Boy stopped outside a busy café and looked in at the young people sitting inside. "I've never seen such beautiful girls in all my life," he said innocently. "Where did you expect to see beautiful girls—in your village? You'd be lucky to see a cow where you come from!" joked Xhemal with the urbanity of someone who has just stepped off the last flight from JFK. Everyone burst out laughing. But they soon sobered up when they saw a black man kissing a blonde girl. "You see," said one of the drivers, "that nigger's got cash; he's not broke like us." The other driver advised him to forget about the "nigger" and concentrate on finding some work. But Xhemal again found a chance to continue the discussion by saying that the wives of rich men are always gagging for black men and immigrants because there aren't any real men in the West because they all sleep with each other so the women get neglected. Sex Boy was following this conversation eagerly, and judging by his expression looked as though his head was literally spinning. One of the drivers, the one who had wondered why Enver Hoxha had been visited on the Albanians and not the Greeks, insisted on completing the puzzle by explaining that economic wellbeing destroys men in the end, making them soft, like women, and gave an original interpretation, according to which only Albanian men, however well they may live, could never become effeminate, because first of all they are all so sex-starved, and secondly, and more significantly, their DNA is far too masculine for that to be a possibility.

Sex Boy suddenly sprung to life with one of his unexpected contributions, wanting to tell us a joke. "This Albanian socialist, a proletarian, arrives in the next world and meets Skanderbeg, the national hero. Skanderbeg asks him how his descendants are getting on, and the proletarian answers that they're not doing that great, really, as they work all the time and are paid a pittance—but worse than that, they're sex-starved and aren't getting any action. They're desperate for women. He explains that the nomenklatura has as much sex as it wants but the proletariat is permanently frustrated. Skanderbeg is sad to hear this and asks if they at least manage to get in some quality masturbation? 'No. Not even that,' replies the proletarian. 'You see, the Party slogan is "Building Socialism with a gun in one hand and a pickaxe in the other," so we always have our hands full.""'

You've Got a Weird Name

You train yourself to learn people's names quickly, but they never learn yours. They can never remember it. Or, to be frank, they don't like the fact that you've got that strange, difficult, foreign name. Sometimes, without even asking you, they give you a name of their choosing, to make life easier for themselves, to restore order and harmony. "I'll call you Giannis," the tradesman you're working with announces, "so that you can have a decent name too, at last, like everybody else." And you go along with it, just like that, in the same way that people accept their fate. Because you want to be liked by those around you at any cost and have learned that foreign names are appealing only when tourists have them. You are not a tourist, you are a supplicant. In the final analysis, you say to yourself, that's what people are like round here; this is what they do and I have to adapt. Because if you don't, you'll never make it. And you recall your initial oath: I have to make it. From now on, you might have two names, your given name and your immigrant name. One for here and one for there. And the one for here, and maybe forever, is Immigrant.

19

*I*t seemed that everything was going Sex Boy's way that day. We hadn't taken five steps when we found ourselves standing outside a video club. We had never seen anything like it, except on TV. The truth is that even though we were amazed by everything we were seeing, what stunned us more than anything else were the kiosks and the hawkers working the town, bellowing down their megaphones. The kiosks struck us as completely surreal, so much so that Xhemal wondered why nobody robbed them. "If this was Albania, they'd be empty." Anyway, we charged into the video club as though we had come to greet the Messiah. Inside there was only the one assistant, a dark-haired, really gorgeous young woman. When she saw the invasion, all of us dressed in what were effectively rags, black with filth and exhaustion, with uncombed hair, she was terrified. She leapt to her feet and took a step back. She didn't even ask what we wanted, she just stared at us, as though she were waiting for us to attack her or make off with all the videos. Sex Boy was in his element. He had discovered the porn section and was inspecting the covers one by one, back and front, the way that an archaeologist might examine the bones of a dinosaur. If we hadn't literally pulled him out, he could happily have spent at least another week in there.

Back outside, Xhemal and the drivers walked a short distance ahead and Sex Boy and I followed them. Sex Boy, transformed by his experience inside the video club, had suddenly become very talkative and *started telling me the valium story. Apparently he'd managed to buy a special hi-tech device from a man in his town that allowed you to watch foreign channels, many more than a standard antenna can pick up, including a couple of porn channels that you could get late at night. Unfortunately his house was very small and he couldn't turn on the TV at that hour without waking up his parents, who slept in the next room. Once his father did wake up and saw what his son was watching, all hell broke loose. But since Sex Boy could not resist temptation, he had to come up with a solution to the parent problem: he bought some valium, which he sneaked into his parents' food at dinner time every evening. His father got a double dose, just to be sure that Sex Boy could enjoy an uninterrupted night of pleasure with his favorite films. But his father soon got suspicious about the fact that he and his wife were suddenly sleeping so deeply and were finding it so difficult to wake up in the morning for work. One evening, the father proved himself to be a little more cunning than the son. He pretended to have eaten his dinner, but actually flushed it down the toilet. What happened next is something Sex Boy would rather forget: he'd been caught redhanded; the special hi-tech device was history and he got the thrashing of his life.*

Through listening to the valium story I also found out what Sex Boy's real name was. He was called Marenglen, a portmanteau name made up of three sainted names: Marx, Engels, and Lenin.

It's Worse at Night

You change your name. You get baptized. You learn the language, unusual words, colloquial expressions, the former to charm your audience, the latter to prove that you are the same as everybody else. But you still feel foreign, very foreign, extremely foreign, a regular outsider.

It's worse at night. First news item: A gang of Albanians have raped and murdered a seventy-year-old woman. Second item: horrific crime in the suburbs. Police warn Albanians might be responsible, followed by a statement from a police officer: "Looking for Albanian criminals is like looking for a needle in a haystack." Third item: Masked burglars, most probably Albanians, broke into a house in Peristeri, threatened an elderly couple with axes and knives, and robbed them. And you ask yourself, how could they possibly have identified them, since their faces were hidden under balaclavas? Never mind. And then there's a special report on crime among immigrants, mostly Albanians, with the soundtrack of a Dario Argento film playing in the background, followed by a bit of Wagner. The reporter enumerates all the crimes committed by Albanians, or "most likely" committed by Albanians, and in a tone reminiscent of frontline war reporting, cries, "We are nursing a time bomb that has already been detonated, and will go off any minute. Everybody and everything has been looted and plundered. They murder, rob, rape, spreading fear everywhere. These are extremely dangerous people. But enough is enough. Deport them, now. Please. This is the will of the people. Albanian immigrants are a scourge. They must leave now. They burgle people's country houses, they break into people's homes, take the lead role in most robberies; they'd kill you for your loose change." Cut—the reporter goes off the air. So does the Dario Argento music.

20

*B*efore Sex Boy had time to finish his story, we found ourselves standing in front of a supermarket. The drivers didn't want to go in. They were keeping their eyes peeled for building sites and opportunities for work. Xhemal, Sex Boy, and I all wanted to go in, and in the end all five of us did. It wasn't a very big supermarket, but it was the first supermarket any of us had ever seen. We didn't have any money to buy anything, so we just walked up and down the aisles, admiring not so much the goods on sale but the bounty and the freedom of choice. We wandered around in speechless admiration, each of us lost in his own world. The other shoppers and the staff looked at us, too, sometimes with curiosity, sometimes with pity and sometimes with fear. At one point I noticed Xhemal at the shampoo and perfume section. I don't know how long we stayed there before we eventually decided to leave.

Our exit was somewhat eventful, because on the way out the staff told us to come through the checkout. We told them we hadn't bought anything, at which two men appeared, rounded us up into a corner and told us to wait. Xhemal in particular looked impatient and suggested running for it, but the drivers said the supermarket would have the police on us in no time and we'd be in deep shit if they did. We stood there for a few minutes until a couple of men in uniform arrived. We *immediately took them to be policemen. They looked at us with suspicion and told us to put our arms in the air. We all realized that we were about to be searched, and one of the drivers started to protest, but checked himself; most likely because he thought he was dealing with the police. The people in the shop were staring at us as though they were watching a short film about some aliens that had suddenly landed in their local supermarket. The "policemen" searched us, stuffed their hands into our jackets and pockets in the hope of finding something, and when they didn't, let us leave.*

The minute we got outside, the drivers reminded us that they had been right not to want to go in: look what happened—those animals in uniforms humiliated us in public for no reason. I was expecting Xhemal to chip in as usual with some kind of anticommunist remark, but he didn't. Instead he was wearing an expression that was somewhere between cynicism and smugness, and said, "Back in Albania, my friend, this would have had an entire regiment of women eating out of your hand," and held up the bottle of perfume he'd stolen from the supermarket. Before we could work out what had happened back there, one of the drivers starting swearing at Xhemal, telling him that he'd come to Greece to find work, not to shoplift. Things became very heated when Xhemal called him an asshole, arguing that one stolen bottle of perfume wasn't going to put the supermarket owner out of business. One insult followed another until the two of them came to blows. Xhemal started it, kicking the driver when he insulted Xhemal's mother. We tried to separate them, forming a jumble of bodies, but were quickly brought to our senses when Sex Boy shouted, "Police! Police!"

At a distance of less than 100 meters we could see a patrol car, which had probably seen the fighting, and was coming our way. I don't know who set us off, Xhemal probably, since he had stolen the perfume in the first place and had more to be frightened of than the rest of us—but we all started running for our lives. I can't even be sure that the police car was coming for us. What I do remember is that we ran into a building site and hid, panting from the exercise, terrified that we'd be caught. Then Sex Boy, more impatient than out of breath, turned to Xhemal and asked, "OK, so how come they didn't find it? Where did you hide it?"

Commercial Break

Time for a commercial break: beautiful beaches, expensive cars, sexy women in stilettos, toothpaste, toilet paper, fizzy drinks, life insurance, aftershave, women's underwear unfurling in the sky in time to Chopin's Waltz opus 64, No 1. An angelic world, gentle and perfectly proportioned, fast-paced at bargain prices with expensive cars, all easily accessible with amazing mobile phones and perfect English, with multiple personas you change as often as you would your shirt, with late nights, sex and alcohol. In this wonderland, which consumes at a dizzying rate and with dizzying ease, you feel that you and your origins are the only things out of place.

Something's not quite right, you think, somewhere down the line something has gone wrong, things get tricky, tough and merciless. Why should I have to answer for every last criminal who happens to have been born in the same country as me? I can only answer for myself, maybe for those closest to me, at a pinch: my brother, my parents who haven't got a bad bone in their bodies, who've never harmed anyone. Everybody should be answerable for their own actions, and that's why the cards seem fixed and stacked against you from the start. They want me to feel guilty, a victim at any cost, even though I haven't done anything.

If you are guilty, you have no rights, only duties and your first duty is to feel inferior, always—and different, grateful that you're allowed to exist at all. You sit there frozen, the remote control in your hand. You turn off the television. You don't know whether to weep or wail. You get the urge to bite, something, anything, the TV screen, the remote, yourself. Then you recall those lyrics you read somewhere, but you can't remember who wrote them: "I wonder if you remember / the broken teeth of love / which from sadness and hunger / bit the stars?"

21

I can't say how long we were hiding out in the building site. The atmosphere was tense, not so much because of the police car—we weren't even sure it was following us—but because of the fight between Xhemal and one of the drivers. We eventually emerged from the site, and our original plan, to return to Igoumenitsa for the night and resume our search for work the following morning, was no longer practical. We were scared of getting into trouble with the police. We were starving, and the drivers, the only ones who had any money, offered to buy everyone something to eat. Even though one of them had been fighting with Xhemal, he was still included in the offer. We got to a shop. The drivers went in and came out carrying sandwiches, which, hungry as we were, seemed to us an irresistible feast, and Xhemal found another opportunity for cursing the mothers of communism and Enver Hoxha, respectively.

The cold was getting unbearable, more so after the sandwiches. Because of this, we all agreed to return to the refugee center; it wasn't as if we had any other options. With much difficulty, we found the bus stop and were in for another long wait, as we had no idea when the bus was due. It arrived eventually and we got on—different conductor this time. He asked us to pay for our tickets, and we came back with the same answer, "Albania fukara, Albania refugiat." This conductor also got annoyed, but didn't threaten to kick us off like the previous one *had. This time I didn't suggest that the drivers consider paying for our tickets. Now and again I exchanged the odd word with Sex Boy, while the two drivers sat there looking pensive and said nothing. Even Xhemal looked thoughtful. We had set off for Igoumenitsa convinced we'd find work, and were returning with nothing more than a body search in a supermarket, with two of us having got into a fight over a stolen bottle of perfume, which, according to Xhemal, would have had an entire regiment of women eating out of your hand back in Albania.*

We eventually got back to the warehouse. An almost identical scene to the one we'd left: soldiers, policemen, and Albanian fugitives standing in a line. While we had been wandering around Igoumenitsa in the freezing cold, there were more arrivals, quite a lot of new arrivals, with the result that the population in the warehouse had swollen and it was very difficult to get through. The new ones told us stories, stories that made your hair stand on end. Some were saying that the Albanian soldiers were opening and closing the borders at will and would take pot shots at the fugitives for the fun of it, and at other times would let people through unchallenged. Some were talking about mass murder, while others were saying that the soldiers were no longer taking orders from their superiors, and to avoid murdering people, had started to desert en masse. Some of the new ones had crossed very hazardous terrain, full of snow, wolves, and chasms. They pointed to a group of very young men who had lost one of their friends during the crossing. He was only eighteen. The rest of them had survived by a miracle. There were five or six of them, sitting together, tired and worn out, in silence. Other people were telling stories about wolves attacking exhausted fugitives, tearing them to pieces. The latest piece of information was that a few fugitives had left the refugee center and made their way to Athens, to a big square, where you could find work immediately. We discussed the idea ourselves: Xhemal, Sex Boy, and I were all for it, but the drivers insisted that we should stay put, because we would definitely find work if we did.

We relaxed a little when Sex Boy, who had a talent for finding out the latest and most accurate news from the warehouse, told us that one of the new arrivals was someone who was a bit soft in the head, and had become the only light entertainment for the fugitives. The madman was 100 percent sure, and he told everybody this in confidence, that he was George Bush's nephew, and that President Bush was in fact an Albanian, and came from the village of Dardhë e Vogël, or Small Pear, somewhere close to the Greek border. Bush's nephew was promising everyone that he would have a word with his uncle and ask him to send a big airplane that would take everyone to America right away. This was the last piece of information I got that night. I was so shattered I fell asleep without realizing it and still cannot work out how I found any room to lie down amid the rabble.

The Small Screen: From Fan to Hostage

You learned the language so that you wouldn't stick out any more, but you were only shooting yourself in the foot in the end. Because it is now that you really feel utterly and completely foreign. If you didn't know the language, at least you'd be spared everything they say on the news. Now you understand everything. Watching television has turned into an exercise in masochism, and you watch a lot of television because you're on your own and don't go out much. Lonely people who don't go out much watch a lot of television.

Television used to be the pre-eminent source of your fantasies, the only window through which you could escape and travel in your imagination, dreaming of magical, forbidden worlds: the West, freedom, equality, prosperity. You created in your mind a world of harmony and beauty, and with this construct in your head, you crossed the borders.

Television is now the source of all your nightmares. It projects a magnified view of your dissonant, repellent, terrifying face. Your great passion is suddenly your most menacing enemy. "I am not like that," you shout, but your voice does not affect the image. The image, of your repulsive face, is all-powerful, it's everywhere, it multiplies with dizzying speed, meeting minimal resistance along the way because it puts it to people in the most simplistic of terms: absolute good versus absolute evil; native versus foreigner. And it sticks, because it does not challenge the human mind, it panders to the most primitive narcissism and speaks to the most primitive fears. And there's nothing you can do about it because in this relentless theater the part allotted to you is that of absolute evil, blackness, the foreigner. There is nothing you can do about it. You have no voice. You are not even a consumer. All those amazing products and goods that are paraded before you after the news are out of your reach: you can't buy them, and that makes you absolutely n-o-t-h-i-n-g. And then the world starts to assume, perhaps for the first time, its real dimensions. Demythologizing begins. Then you start to miss the fresh air, and the tears well up in your eyes, while your brain is banging out that phrase nobody has ever said and nobody is ever likely to come out and say in public: "You are n-o-t-h-i-n-g, n-o-t-h-i-n-g, n-o-t-h-i-n-g."

22

I woke up the next morning with my head on a stranger's thigh while the head of another stranger was resting on my leg. My entire body was stiff. I was freezing cold and shaking all over. Someone had lit a fire inside the warehouse to get warm. The cold pierced right through your bones. They were taking a risk because if the Greek police spotted it, they would go berserk. I started to move cautiously, trying not to wake either the man above me or the man underneath me. I was partially successful, and moved across to the fire. The men around it seemed to have just arrived and were sleeping in a sitting position. I looked around for a familiar face and eventually spotted Sex Boy. He was awake and told me that he hadn't been able to get any sleep. He had found somewhere to lie down but was complaining bitterly about two men who stank and who weren't just snoring but were braying, so much so, according to Sex Boy, that they could have raised the dead, who would have instantly fled to escape the noise. We both agreed that the warehouse resembled a pigsty more than anything else, and if things went on like this, we'd soon be ridden with fleas and disease.

While all of this was going on, I'd woken up with a rather strange idea: I wanted to see what a bookshop in the West looked like. Books were my great passion. I hadn't managed to see a bookshop when we were in Igoumenitsa because the rest of the group had other priorities. I confided this ambition in Sex Boy. 'Why didn't you mention it yesterday?

We were walking around the town for hours!" He finally gave in because he was just as keen as I was to escape the hellish atmosphere of the warehouse and would be hard-pressed to find better company than mine.

"The cold outside has to be better than this—at least there won't be any germs," he concluded, so off we went into the village in search of a Western bookshop. As I hadn't the faintest idea where it could be, I asked two young boys in a mixture of Italian and English. They struggled to tell me which general direction we should go in.

Before we started our search, we decided to go into a café to get warm. There were only a few people inside and a waiter who didn't even take the trouble to ask us what we wanted. It looked like he was used to people coming in just to warm up and not order anything. Sex Boy and I talked a bit, in hushed voices, in Albanian, until the waiter came over to us, carrying a tray with two cups of tea on it. He spoke to us in Greek, and pointed across to the other side of the café at an old gentleman. We worked out that the tea was his treat. We thanked him with the traditional gesture, placing the right hand close to the heart. He responded with a sweet smile and returned the gesture. "We and the Greeks belong to the same tribe," said Sex Boy, sipping his tea. Since we had the privilege of drinking tea we fancied ourselves regular customers, and therefore had the right to stay there a little longer, get a little bit warmer, and to give the sun a chance to warm up a bit as well. And that's what we did. We left with a proud "efharisto," which seemed to please the waiter a great deal, and resumed our search, this time in the best of spirits, for the Western bookshop. Eventually Sex Boy and I did come across something like a bookshop, which to me at that moment was something quite sublime.

A Tough Life

Immigrant, alien, supplicant: your profession is all these things. Your life is a tough one, because you don't want to go back to where you came from, but you're not wanted here, either. It is tough because if you want to find work, you'll have to change your name. It is tough because you'll always be persona non grata. It is tough because when you got sick that day, and were running a fever of 102, and couldn't go to work, your boss sacked you just like that. It is tough because when you ask for a bit more, it's called hubris, but when your employer pays you just one tenth of the basic wage for twelve, thirteen, fourteen hours of working like a dog, he's being kind, he's doing you a favor. It is tough because for you there are three things that are sacrosanct: work, sex, and a residence permit—and you'd happily trade sexual passion for a residence permit. It is tough because the police can catch you whenever they want to, swear at you as much as they want to, and hold you at the station for as long as they want to. Your bitter moniker for the police, the *astynomia* (civil guard) is *astronomia* (guards of the stars) because your fate on this earth so often depends on them. A tough life because some of your fellow countrymen commit crimes, and when they do you have to keep out of the way of the Black Marias on Operation Sweep-up, and out of the way of the TV cameras that just love Operation Hatred and Misinformation. One newspaper shouts, "Albanians out!" while another declares, "Albanians are the most disgusting race on earth." It is tough because stealing one watermelon is enough for someone to kill you and get away with murder.

It's a tough life because in many cases the police fire warning shots to scare you and somehow manage to get you in the back of your head with uncanny mathematical precision. Afterward the policeman gets off and nobody loses any sleep over it. It's a tough life because if you want to rent a flat you have to sweat for it much more than the average Olympic gold medalist weightlifter does. You change your name, you watch your accent, give your best linguistic self, and if you still don't make it, you change your nationality and your religion, too. You become a Romanian, a Serb, a Russian, because deep down you are all those nationalities and they are all you. It's a tough life because you are young and full of love, and when the local girls find out you are Albanian they instantly evaporate and you risk (don't laugh) spending your life without a lover. It's a tough life because they have declared you a modern-day cannibal. The zealous cameras zoom in on the crimes you commit (when they aren't fabricating them, that is), but never catch the blatant exploitation that pushed you to crime in the first place, and never notice the benefits you bring to the local economy, and always miss the enormous profits you bring your boss. That's why we hear people talking about you so much but never saying anything nice about you. It's a tough life because there are so many opportunities for becoming neurotic and miserable, and for being consumed by loneliness every single day. Loneliness, as a poet once said, is not missing other people but finding yourself in a big crowd, talking, and not being understood. There are so many opportunities for becoming suspicious and aggressive toward those you have become convinced don't want you. In this way you slide into the underbelly of society, where there is more than enough darkness, and where the greatest danger of all lurks: that you will give in to this darkness.

I'll stop here because you're tired and need your sleep. Another tough day awaits you. But if I've made you smile at any stage at your own sufferings, you know better than anyone that scapegoat humor is only a temporary gift, on loan from heaven to hell.

23

*F*ortunately *for me there was someone in the bookshop wanting to buy a paper or a book, I couldn't really work out which, who spoke French. We got talking and he showed me where to find the books by García Márquez, there were two or three, as well as one by Borges, which I'd managed to read on the sly in Italian. I was entranced by my conversation with him, and began to feel that I had landed somewhere between the Library of Alexandria and the Sistine Chapel until a hand grabbed me by the collar from behind and demanded, in broken Albanian, "Ermi babai?" Everything happened in a matter of seconds. I saw the terrified look on the face of the person I'd been talking to, and the body of a police officer pulling me with tremendous force out of the shop. I was panic-stricken. I started screaming and shouting, begging the man I'd been talking to for help, insisting I was innocent. Quite what I was innocent of he didn't know either, but when a policeman grabs you by the collar, shouting, it's obvious you're about to be accused of something. The officer dragged me outside, still screaming. That's when I saw Sex Boy down on the ground, another policeman bending over him and thrashing him with his truncheon. I also saw the Black Maria they were taking us to. While my Francophone friend tried to talk to the policeman, I carried on screaming and by now the second policeman had ditched his truncheon and was pulling and kicking Sex Boy to his feet. At some point, they threw us into the Black Maria. Sex Boy was sitting next to me, terrified* *out of his wits, and said to me in a shaky voice, "I think they're going to kill us." I didn't have the slightest idea what was going on. It seemed that Sex Boy was destined to get into trouble: wherever he went he made people angry: the café owner, the police, supermarket security guards, everyone. I was reassured slightly by the sight of the sports stadium and our warehouse. Policemen and soldiers were screaming. Something very serious must have happened. I looked for Xhemal and the drivers, but it was difficult to walk through that huge crowd of people packed together like sardines. Sex Boy's face was screwed up in pain, from all the truncheon blows he'd received back at the Western bookshop.*

Resurrecting Memories

One of your crimes is that you remind the natives of what life used to be like for them. They had just started to put all that behind them, bury it in the depths of Lethe, all the pain and humiliation of being an immigrant, the worn-out faces, the peasant gait, the heavy stench of sweat and garlic, the fear of hunger and penury, of being the unbearable "dirty foreigner," *dreckiger Ausländer* in Germany, the sale race in France, dirty Greeks in America, *svartskallar* in Sweden, and so on. Then you come along looking like something out of a photograph taken over fifty years ago.

On the subject of photographs, Leon Pantoti is someone I'm sure you've never heard of. He's an immigrant too. Or was. Leon Pantoti is the name he was issued with at Ellis Island, where all new arrivals in America were naturalized. Unlike most Greeks who arrived in America, Pantoti was not illiterate. He also had a trade: he was a photographer. He quickly learned English and opened a studio in San Francisco, photographing Greeks and Americans between 1914 and 1922. Portraits of children, mothers, laborers, rich and poor, bachelors and newlyweds, mail-order brides shipped out from Greece, because the local women were out of reach to the average immigrant. He photographed beautiful foreign girls who married elderly locals, usually for their money or a residence permit, or both. In one such picture taken by Pantoti the bride is showing off her right leg, trying to look flirtatious and give an impression of the comfortable existence she had just embarked on. The photograph has everything in it: dreams, pretense, harsh reality, comedy—because being an immigrant is all those things.

This pose must seem faintly absurd to the descendants of the bride, American citizens today. Isn't the same thing going to happen when your descendants see a picture of you, when you tell your own child, who will grow up in Greece, all about how you originally furnished your home with the broken chairs and armchairs people chucked out onto the pavement and how gratefully you collected them from the "immigrants" supermarket, otherwise known as the trash heap? Your son will say, "Daddy! You were a beggar—how embarrassing!"

Immigrant existence goes in cycles. So does the look on its face. It doesn't just have one look, it has several. For the first generation there's that neurotic look of the orphan: "Which country do I really belong to?" Then there's the look of the immigrant who makes it: pride and vanity. And then there's the look of the immigrant who doesn't make it, the look of failure and plenty of resentment. The look of the locals looking at immigrants is usually out of range. At first it's full of sympathy, then it becomes puzzled before it turns suspicious and worried when it sees that yesterday's barefooted man wants to become like him, resemble him, and perhaps even do better than him.

24

*T*hey eventually let us out of the Black Maria and herded us with the help of their truncheons into the warehouse. We started looking for our friends, and after much difficulty we located the two drivers. We asked them what was going on but even they weren't sure, because some people were saying that some of us had raped a Greek girl in the village while others claimed that a priest had groped an Albanian man who responded by beating him up and shaving him. Another version was that a well-known lout from Tirana had punched a policeman; others insisted that the truth was actually much simpler. It was market day in Filiates and some of our number were strolling through the stalls, demonstrating to the traders there what it means to acquire goods without paying for them. A group stormed into a small shop and literally emptied it of all its Cokes and beers while the shop owner looked on in frozen disbelief. It was said that this event spread fear and panic among local traders and shopkeepers and that the villagers demanded that the police round up the Albanians and establish order.

It was impossible to work out what had really happened; the police had turned truly savage. They were swearing, pounding the wire in front of our warehouse, and refusing to let anyone leave. By way of punishment they didn't give us anything to eat that day or the next. Cold, lack of sleep, and now starvation. Some of the villagers would try to throw us a crust or two over the railings but were rewarded with the fury of the police *for their pains. The warehouse had been converted into a prison: we were only allowed to relieve ourselves right next to the warehouse, not a step further. Somewhere close to all the shit was the tap we were supposed to drink water out of. Some of us started saying that they were going back to Albania, because at least there was a bed waiting for them at home, but most people insisted that there was no turning back. "After forty-five years waiting to cross the border it would be a shame to stay for such a short time, wouldn't it?"*

Through all this chaos, Sex Boy brought us the main story of the day: in addition to the mad Albanian who was threatening the police that he was going to report them to his uncle, George Bush, there was another guest star, a mute. But he was no ordinary mute. He was not an Albanian mute. He was a Greek mute, unlucky enough to get caught up in the police round-up. Because he couldn't speak, they took him for another Albanian and threw him into the warehouse along with the rest of us. The Albanian crowd had spotted the mistake and took special care of him. I don't how they managed it in this horrendous chaos, but they got hold of a pen and a piece of paper, and somebody who knew Greek was able to communicate with the mute. Before long almost everyone had learned his name. He was called Dimitris. Dimitris was a farmer. He had left home that morning without his ID, which is how he ended up in our warehouse as he had not been able to speak and his face left the police with the unshakeable impression that he was Albanian. Some attempts were made to persuade them that there had been a mistake, but the police were not in a mood to listen that day, and the negotiators were in danger of getting beaten up if they pushed it too much. They eventually gave up, and Dimitris had to spend the night in the warehouse with the rest of us, though his anxiety probably kept him awake most of the night.

Even Albanians are Getting Expensive

Thursday. The evening news. The cameras fall on farmland and farm workers, Greeks as well as migrants, somewhere in Larissa, then somewhere in Crete. The news item is brief:

"Albanian immigrant workers demand wage increase." The caption flashing across the bottom of the screen reads: "Even Albanians are getting expensive!" Just imagine the journalist responsible for that one, sitting in front to his computer screen, trying to squeeze a catchy caption out of his brain. That is truly inspired. Worth its weight in gold, and with it he's finished another tiring day at the network. The truth is, copywriters are just another sector of the workforce struggling to make ends meet, and in all likelihood this one isn't paid or rewarded much for his work. He might even be the Albanian of the media industry. "Even Albanians are getting expensive," much as you'd say, "Even potatoes have gone up." It's that microscopic, seemingly innocuous little "even" that does all the work. It establishes the distance between natives and immigrants, between those who have the right to try to improve their lot and those who don't, between yesterday's immigrants and today's immigrants.

The copywriter probably hadn't given it that much thought. He'd probably never heard of, let alone read the story of his compatriot, the Ludlow martyr, Louis Tikas.[4]

Tikas lead the Greek miners' strike in Colorado at the beginning of the twentieth century. Louis Tikas wasn't his real name; he was called Ilias Anastassiou Spantoudakis, but changed it to Tikas to get American citizenship. He was murdered by hired killers put onto him by the bosses because he refused to let Greek immigrants back down from their demands for higher wages and better working conditions.

Much of the local press back then poured scorn on the Greeks, because up to this point they had been the cheapest labor around, and were sometimes used by their bosses as strikebreakers, and then suddenly, there they were, also wanting to be expensive. They were doused in various epithets such as *"arrivistes,"* "coffee drinkers," "bloodthirsty," and *"den katalavenees"* (he doesn't understand). These young men, most of them from agricultural backgrounds, lived in fear of the landslides inside the mines and lived in fear of amputations, but their greatest fear of all was the fear of failure. They had left home and their country for money, not security. The only education they had received consisted of a few popular sayings, a couple of dozen songs about vendettas and wars with the Turks, the poem "Erotokritos," and the odd folk ballad.

Most of them—the ones that didn't die in the mines, that is—stayed on in America. A few, a tiny minority, returned to Greece. The descendants of these rough, illiterate Greek immigrants did make it: they became American citizens, businessmen, politicians, renowned university professors, and some of them today even spend a lot of time digging up the stories of their ancestors.

Who knows whether after eighty years some descendant of the peasant immigrants of today, from Albania or India, won't be doing the same thing? And perhaps, while looking into his forefathers' experience, he'll stumble across that "even," which might give him an idea for the title of the book he's planning: *Even Albanians Are Getting Expensive*. The irony is that thanks to those immigrants, their faces worn with exhaustion and too much exposure to the sun, the copywriter who penned this catchy legend might just have earned a footnote in the history books.

25

We all woke up the next morning hoping that the fury of the policemen had subsided. It hadn't. The police had surrounded the warehouse with even more wire fencing to stop people getting out. The focus of the entire morning was Dimitris, the Greek mute who had been mistaken for an Albanian. He had written down something in Greek on a piece of paper, which we were desperately trying to pass on to the police so that they would know that there was a Greek in our midst. From what I could gather, he'd written his name, surname, and the name of his village, and the words I AM GREEK in larger letters underneath. The police gradually got wind of what had happened, although it took some convincing for them to accept that it wasn't just another Albanian scam. About ten policemen came into the warehouse late in the afternoon looking for Dimitris, the Albanian-looking Greek farmer. They found him easily because the rest of us immediately realized why they'd come. They seized him by the arms and marched him out as though they had just made an arrest. Dimitris was never heard of again. I suspect that the only thing that came of all this was the two-fold satisfaction felt by the residents of the warehouse: first of all from the police blunder and secondly, this episode had proved that a Greek could easily pass for an Albanian, so by extension an Albanian must be able to pass for a Greek.

But our biggest concern at that point was our hunger, and the fact that the authorities appeared to have absolutely no intention of feeding us. In a united show of protest, we all started stamping our feet and shouting rhythmically, "duam bukë, duam bukë, duam bukë"—*"we want bread, we want bread, we want bread." The chorus of voices was quite impressive, and the warehouse started vibrating from all the sad music. We must have repeated this chant more than ten times, and in addition to expressing our feeling of extreme hunger, this was a civilized way for us to spend our time, as one of the drivers pointed out. Eventually we were heard. After nightfall, ten policemen clutching their truncheons in one hand and large sacks in the other strode into the warehouse. They screamed out orders for us to get down on our knees, which we did. They opened the sacks and started pulling out loaves of bread, and throwing them randomly around while the starving recipients fought like maniacs over them. I saw the two drivers fighting with all their strength over the same loaf, the same two men who only three days earlier had been convinced that they were en route to Germany to work the Berlin–Baghdad route for an astronomical wage. When the policemen left war broke out, a real bread war. In among the fray, a very big, bulky character had, for reasons best known to himself, grabbed George Bush's nephew by the throat, and would have surely killed him had not a few slightly calmer men pulled him off. Fortunately, at some point order restored itself. It was then that I felt someone touching my back. It was the two drivers, ecstatically happy, giving me a flash of their booty, which they'd hidden under a jacket: three whole loaves of bread. This gave me a chance to appease my hunger, as I'd stayed out of the bread war. Naturally the mood of the crowd was as uneven as a rudderless ship travelling through an almighty storm, sometimes disappearing beneath the furious waves, only to reappear later on the crest.*

Half an hour later, once people had eaten, we heard singing: a love song. A small group at the other end of the warehouse had started it and gradually everybody joined in singing what resembled a compulsory protest song. We'd gone from singing "We want bread" to "Oh! Nightingale in Spring:"[5] Ore bilbil ç'ta kam bërë benë / vetëm mos të gjeça mor I pabesë folenë / do të marrë dhe do të hedh nëlumë / se na I le çupat more çapkën pa gjumë / hidhesh e përdridhesh porsi gjarpri / si t'ja bëj unë I varfëri. *Everybody was singing, and those who didn't know the words sang along with a "na, na, na." The fact that such a sweet love song was being sung at that moment by a huge crowd of people in a very aggressive mood made it sound like a war song. I asked myself whether hungry people were capable of singing love songs any other way. The police outside must have thought the Albanians had gone mad. I wanted to share my thoughts with one of the drivers, but he had given himself completely to the mood of the song and there, in the half-light, I could make out the tears running down his cheeks.*

The Scapegoat of the Poor

The rich don't usually mind you. Those who fear you the most are those who read few books but watch plenty of television. Those who send their children to the same school as yours, who live in the same neighborhood, who wait in the same lines as you at the health insurance offices at dawn. Those who worry about sinking to your level, becoming like the Albanians. They latch onto national stereotypes with zeal, any stereotypes for that matter, because they don't want to lose that divine distance between superior and inferior. It's the only thing that makes them feel that they are not at the bottom of the heap. There is nothing worse than the disgust one poor devil shows another. It provides fertile waters for politicians to go fishing for votes as they scream for a country free of immigrants, selling fear and resentment, and spreading the false impression that immigrants are the root of the nation's problems. They will convince voters that if only you had the decency to go back to where you came from, they would be eating from golden spoons. That if you hadn't come in the first place, they would be at work and prosperous, their children wouldn't be at drugs, and they would be able to go to sleep with the windows open at night. And thus, with the promise of open windows, the poor retreat into this simplistic logic, the logic of resentment and xenophobia. It's an age-old game: the rich are responsible for coming up with racist theories, and it's the job of the poor to apply them by pursuing other poor people, and thus the poor get poorer and the rich get richer.

26

*B*ecause we felt that the conditions in the warehouse were intolerable and were an insult, some of us took the initiative to organize a kind of general meeting. A self-appointed committee started to summarize the situation of the last few days. "We are treated like animals even though the European Union has given the Greeks billions for us," announced one impassioned member. Everyone around him burst into applause. One of the drivers, who was sitting close to me whispered, "Look at us now. What big boys—who could guess we've been applauding the Party for the last fifty years?" I said nothing, just smiled. I followed the scene, feeling like I was watching something straight out of the theater of the absurd. After the first speech, which had whipped everyone into a frenzied fighting spirit, the decision was made to send a letter of protest to the UN. Everyone was convinced that the UN had nothing to occupy itself with other than the terrible fate of Albanian refugees in Greece. They were equally convinced that as soon as our letter reached them, they'd send out economic aid and our troubles would be over once and for all. Initial joy turned to enthusiasm; enthusiasm, to delirium. Everyone agreed, and decided that the protest letter should be written right away and sent with no time to lose. The difficulty was that there was only one pen and no more paper; all the paper had been used for Dimitris. But the most serious obstacle was that nobody had a postal address for the UN, or indeed knew where there was a mailbox in

Filiates, and even if we did, the police would never let us go to it. There was no discussion about the language the letter should be written in. And that's how we spent our third night in the warehouse, writing a fantasy protest letter addressed to the UN.

The Neurosis of Staying On

You used to say: "As soon as I've saved up enough money, I'll go home." Many years later, you're still saying the same thing. You used to say: "I'll move on to another country, where I'll earn better money and live better." You stayed here. The truth is that the idea of leaving has become second nature. You are always somewhere between eternal flight and eternal return. You are, as always, full of contradictions, and you want to compromise where there can be no compromise. That's the way the game goes when you're away from home. It's relentless and only for those with nerves of steel. Anyone who's tried walking along the shifting sands the immigrant walks on knows that. It's the neurosis that comes with staying on. One day you're saying, "I'm going back, I can't stand being away any more; it's unbearable here," and the next day it's, "I'll stay a bit longer, get a bit more money together," and the day after that you're all, "I have to make it here."

Even though people generally do stay in the first country they migrate to, you'll always be a permanent fugitive. So much so that I wonder if it isn't some kind of unconscious strategy, a lifestyle choice made by those who suffer from Border Syndrome; perhaps it's all nothing more than a form of self-defense, because you never know whether you'll make it or not, or whether you'll put down roots here in the country you chose to come to. That's why you keep those two contradictory scenarios in reserve: to remain or to return? Like an emergency exit from insecurity and your fear that perhaps they won't let you put down roots here.

Most likely you'll stay put. You have very few chances of going back, and deep down you know that, because you're beginning to realize that you are more of a foreigner back home than you are here. An immigrant is like a tree: his branches face his homeland, the one he left behind, while his roots grow deeper and deeper into the soil of the country he chose to come to. If you end up being one of a handful that does go back, you'll resemble the ancient immigrant in Ignazio Silone's novel *Bread and Wine*, the peasant everyone in the village called Sciatap, an Italian corruption of "shut up"—apparently the only phrase he'd learned in that country. Shut up. Shut up.

27

*I*t had become impossible to sleep at night. There was no room. The burliest men occupied the foam mats, which functioned as beds and had turned black with filth. The weaker ones waited till morning when some space was vacated by the stronger ones. By now hunger had kicked in and I was extremely weak. I looked at the drivers: they had both lost all their initial enthusiasm and optimism for good. I went over to join them and found them in the middle of a tense discussion, the one blaming the other for the decision to cross the border. "Have you any idea how much the truck we abandoned costs? I was responsible for it, so if they decide to charge me for it, I'll be working it off for the rest of my life," the driver shouted at the codriver.

They were no longer the two drivers but driver and codriver. The codriver said nothing for a while before retorting, "I asked you three times if you really had the bottle for it." Now it was the driver's turn to go quiet.

I asked them if they'd seen Xhemal anywhere. "Xhemal has escaped from the camp," they told me. The refugee center had been referred to as "the camp" for the last two days. How, with whom, or where Xhemal had escaped to they couldn't tell me. All they knew was that he was gone, maybe to Athens, maybe he'd found work in Igoumenitsa at some garage, but they really couldn't say. Sex Boy insisted that he had left with some strange characters and headed for Athens. Xhemal hadn't *said anything to us. The truth is that after the fight with the driver, he had become a bit distant and had started keeping company with other people in the warehouse. Sex Boy, our very own 007, told us that some of them had knives and one had a pistol. We were all shocked because we hadn't noticed anything of the kind. Apparently these men had taken charge of things inside the warehouse and were offering to help people who wanted to escape, for a fee, which could be paid back at a later date, in dollars, drachmas or lek. Sex Boy also told us that the previous night someone who had challenged them and sworn at them got a bad beating for his pains. That was the kind of company Xhemal had chosen to escape with. "That man would have sold his own sister if the price was right, mark my words," said the driver who had fought with him.*

Toward the end of the day we had an unexpected visitor, an elderly priest who arrived with an interpreter in tow. Everyone gathered round to listen: buses were arriving the following morning to take us, in alphabetical order, to various destinations around Greece, where we would be housed and given work. The euphoria this news spread through the warehouse is difficult to describe; some were so excited that they grabbed hold of the priest and threw him up in the air repeatedly, the way soccer players do with their coaches after winning the cup. As they tossed him up and caught him, they chanted, "Papou, papou, papou," forgetting that the priest was an old man, and that in the midst of all the chaos and the shouting, things could go horribly wrong. Five or six policeman entered the fray in order to liberate the priest by opening a corridor down the middle of the room with their truncheons. The released him from the grip of his dangerous fans and escorted him outside. He looked like Christ on Golgotha, but in reality bore a closer resemblance to Judas as he had lied to us over one small detail: the buses were scheduled to arrive; we were expected to wait until our names were called and then get on them, but we were not going to "various destinations around Greece to be housed and given work." The buses were taking us straight back to Albania. This we were only to discover much later.

Your son doesn't speak broken Greek.

Life as an immigrant is a net that you get caught up in without realizing it. It is Cyclops and Ithaca, Circe and Penelope, Scylla and Charybdes, all in one. You learn the language and the customs of the locals without quite understanding how. You change, without wanting to. You learn how to drink your coffee in a different way. Your father's view of the world is full of holes. Unfamiliar streets become part of your day-to-day geography. The locals sometimes praise your knowledge of the language, and of course there are times when you're dying to say, "I didn't learn Greek to please you, I did it for myself." But you don't say it.

This country is slowly beginning to grow on you. There are times when you even love it, without understanding why, and there are other times when you resent it deeply each time you're reminded that you're foreign and each time you're reminded that you're unequal. Each time they refuse to rent out their house to you. But you live here; you work here; your friends are all here and, more to the point, your child is growing up here, growing up thinking himself a native.

He doesn't worry about being let down by his accent; he doesn't have that kind of problem, because he doesn't speak broken Greek like his father does. When people compliment him on his Greek, he just laughs. He doesn't keep out of sight like you used to—he screams and shouts and asserts his presence. He does not take insults with the same resentment you used to. He is not like you. When you suffered rejection, you would slink away to lick your wounds like an injured dog, because you were a foreigner and felt like a foreigner, but he doesn't feel like that. When he's rejected, he doesn't limp off like an injured dog but like an injured wild animal. You would try to treat your neurosis by saying, "One day, I'll go back." For your child this is home. He has no other. He has no choice but to love it or hate it. Whatever it is he has to win or lose he will win or lose here, in the place where you decided he should be brought into the world.

28

*T*he next day the police finally allowed us to go outside onto the soccer field, which had been enclosed by barbed wire all around. Swaggering around, swinging their truncheons, they ordered us to sit down on the steps and wait for our names to be called. We were then to get on the bus that would take us to our destination, where housing and work would be provided. The first fugitives to be called strode up to the bus giving the sign of victory, while the rest of us looked on, green with envy, waiting for our own names to be announced through the megaphone. Two or three busloads left that day; those who weren't called returned to the warehouse disheartened, heads bent and feeling their exhaustion even more keenly. The mysterious glow that had rested on their sullen, tired faces for a few hours had vanished.

That evening ten policemen distributed loaves again, sticking to the tried and tested method: random chucking. This time, however, there were fewer of us and the scramble for food displayed some rudimentary aspects of fair play. Now and again the odd "sorry" and "I didn't mean to hit you" was heard. The drivers had meanwhile become incandescent when they realized their names were not going to be called. Their fury intensified because Sex Boy had made it onto one of the buses, which meant that, according to our collective fantasy, he'd be sleeping in some nicely heated room with an en suite shower. "Bloody hell, that puppy gets to go, while we two, who grew up in the capital, have to stay here!"

protested one of the drivers, obviously forgetting that I was from the provinces, too. I said nothing. They fell silent, realizing a little belatedly how tactless they'd been. I then remembered how Sex Boy had come up to us, hugged us, and told us that as soon as he was sorted he'd do something for us. He was on the verge of tears and for the first time ever I saw in his eyes something resembling joy, something resembling hope.

After a while, with the three of us deep in thought, one of the drivers told us what was at once the funniest and the most tragic story I've ever heard in my life. It was about his cousin, who had been exiled together with her family on account of a fart. Unbelievable but true. It was just after Comrade Enver's death, and the entire nation was obliged to pass by and pay their respects at the tomb of the Eternal Leader. She duly went along with the rest of her collective from the factory where she worked, one of the ones built by the Chinese, in fact. Even though she had a cold that day, she simply had to go, because she couldn't just say she wasn't going at a time when almost all of Albania was making its way to Tirana, even if it meant hanging off those Chinese trains to get there. Compared to the profound sentiment and duty to pay her respects at the tomb of the Eternal Leader, what was a cold if not a sign of bourgeois weakness? The driver's cousin understood only too well that now was not the time to display such infirmities. So she went and waited in the long line, goodness only knows how long for, hours rather than minutes, and when it was eventually her turn, she kneeled down like everyone else, preparing to weep, to sigh and kiss the marble covering the tomb of the Great Leader. However, during the part when she was supposed to emit the customary loud sigh, she instead produced an extremely voluble fart, so distinct and so unmistakable that the person behind her in line heard it and so did the person behind him, both members of the same collective. That was the end of her. They went straight to the Party secretary to report the incident, and the secretary, in view of the solemnity of the occasion, didn't hesitate to call a general meeting to which the cousin was summoned and required to prove that the fart had not been motivated by subversive, hostile aims. The secretary went after her hammer and tongs, *bent on proving her guilt. He argued that the enemy would not hesitate to make use of all means available to him in order to insult the memory of the Eternal Leader and so on and so forth.*

It didn't end there; when they started to sniff around in her past, they discovered that her husband's grandfather had been convicted and executed by the Party in 1948 as a sworn enemy of the Albanian state and of the Party. That was it. How could she possibly hope to convince anyone that her flatulence at the tomb of the Eternal Leader was not somehow connected with the execution of her husband's grandfather? It was a lost cause. Besides, the Party had said it over and over again: water can sleep, enemies never do. Consequently she lost her job and was exiled to a strange village in order to learn how to love the Eternal Leader fittingly in the fields. And thus we passed our fifth night in our warehouse; with the story of the fart. Or was it the sixth? I'd lost track, but at least now we had a bit more room to sleep. I ate a small piece of my loaf and slept like the dead that night.

When They Stop Feeling Sorry for You

There are times when you don't understand your child. He doesn't understand you, either. He doesn't understand your homesickness, and your homeland is nothing but a tourist destination to him. He doesn't feel guilty like you do for having abandoned it. His homeland is here, where he lives. If he feels stigmatized by his origins, he'll probably become neurotic and incapable of loving himself or of loving any country for that matter.

Sometimes your broken Greek embarrasses him; the way you walk embarrasses him; the way you dress embarrasses him; lots of things about you embarrass him. He's not like you, though; he's not an inveterate scrooge desperately saving money in the hope of going back. He wants to dress like the Greek kids, live like them, get on in life like they do, have nice hands like they do, have a career like they do. Heavy manual labor, the kind the Greeks won't touch, is meant for other aliens, the ones who've just arrived. He feels completely at home, which is why he doesn't ask anyone to love him. He knows very well that love is in short supply. He wants his due, that's all: to be treated like an equal, to be judged on his own merits and not on his ethnic background. He wants to make this country his own, because he has no other country to love. If this country rejects him, he'll reject it, too, and he'll be left dangling, much worse off than you because he'll have nowhere to call his own. He'll be a rootless creature ready to embrace an alternative identity—not nostalgia but the ghetto.

Your child doesn't ask to be loved and, above all, he does not ask to be pitied. The pity card that you used to play just to survive is one he despises. Of course he has many more friends than you ever had, and they are gradually accepting him as one of them. But they are slightly more nervous of him than they are of you, mainly because he doesn't inspire pity.

This is when the trouble really starts, when people are no longer able to read any signs of misery and misfortune in his face, when his is no longer pitiful and different, when he starts acting all familiar and making himself at home.

That's when the trouble starts, when the immigrant starts demanding equality. Your child is regularly criticized, not for behaving like a foreigner but for behaving like a Greek. Not because he's different but because he isn't. Because that's when it's clear he's here to stay. The immigrant, dear reader, is tolerated as a temporary extra, but feared and reviled when he looks like he's about to move in for good.

29

*I*t must have been around midday by the time I woke up. The driver woke me. For some reason the police had not brought us outside to sit on the steps and nobody was reading out any lists of names. "Something must have happened," said the codriver. "They're not screaming at us, either." We went outside and saw that he was right. Something had happened, but we couldn't work out what it was. The policemen had abandoned their grim, truncheon-swinging swagger. Not only that, they had actually cleaned up the filth outside the warehouse, and were now calmly asking us to get in line in readiness for a proper midday meal: half a loaf of bread each and some cheese.

Speculation was rife. At first people were claiming that the police had sharpened up after the letter to the UN. Not very likely, considering that the letter, for want of paper, an address and a post office, had never actually been sent. Then it was said that the US ambassador was on his way. Others said it was the British ambassador. By about 2 p.m. it had been agreed that they were both en route but a couple of hours later, there'd apparently been a change of plan: it was a big NATO general, who was recruiting for soldiers to fight in Iraq. George Bush's nephew got into the spirit of things by shrieking every now and then, "Company march!" He'd probably got it from some film he'd seen on Italian TV. The news that we were about to be called up for active service in Iraq caused enormous unrest, and the driver and the codriver were equally incensed, insisting that they *hadn't come to the West to be packed off to fight but to work. By 5 p.m. people had split off into various groups of roughly the same size, according to which of the above scenarios they found most convincing.*

The previous day, out there on the field, I'd struck up a conversation with one of the policemen, in English. I wasn't very good—I'd only got as far as "Essential 2," the most common English language learning method followed in Albania, but the policeman knew even less. His name was Pavlos. He seemed different, not like the other policemen. He didn't shout, he didn't go around wielding his truncheon, and was one of few, or rather the only one, who ever smiled. We'd talked about various things, where I'd come from, what I'd studied back in Albania, while he explained to me that he was originally from Sparta, and I told him I'd read all about the ancient Spartans, the war with Athens, Pericles, and the Acropolis. That day they allowed us to go out for a second time to enjoy what little was left of the winter sun, and I saw him again. To be precise, he saw me first and motioned to me to come over. We got talking again. This time he questioned me more closely about why I'd come, and if I wanted to find work in Greece. I told him that I did, and that I intended to go to university eventually, to study history and philosophy. I also told him that I knew French and Italian. Pavlos was impressed and beckoned me to follow him. We walked along for a while until we got to a group of policemen who were gathered around a man who appeared to be their superior, judging by the way they spoke to him.

Pavlos started talking to him and pointing in my direction. The others listened in silence. Of course I couldn't understand a word of what he was saying, but I could feel the weight of two or three sardonic pairs of eyes on me. Pavlos's little speech was met with a few moments' silence and then his superior responded. He didn't say much, but the single, short phrase he used, coupled with the look on his face, a mixture of boredom and cynicism, was enough to get the rest of them laughing. The cynical stares falling on me multiplied, and Pavlos fell into an embarrassed silence—I saw him turn red. I hadn't been able to follow anything but it was obvious that he'd been completely humiliated. I realized he must have said something about me, something nice, and had been repaid with the sarcasm of his superior and the ridicule of his fellow police officers. I felt myself blushing, too, as though I'd caught the embarrassment from Pavlos. He signaled to me that we should go back, so I followed him. He explained to me that he wasn't like the rest of them and was waiting to start his new job at the airport, as though the policemen at airports were a breed apart. I had to get back inside with the others. Pavlos shook my hand and wished me luck.

The Immigrant's Memory

The immigrant is locked in perpetual dialogue with his memory and with his past. More precisely, he is condemned to be in perpetual opposition to them. Some, several, a great many in fact, faced with this, choose Lethe instead, as a survival strategy or as an inevitable rejection of the state of uprootedness and distance. Once he's rid himself of the past, the immigrant feels much lighter about facing the difficult journey ahead, during which he carries both metaphorical and literal burdens. Being in another country can frequently lead to disengagement with your former self. Now you have the chance to disappear, to settle your scores with your origins, to reinvent yourself, to start a new life from scratch. Some manage, some don't. When this strategy fails, memory comes back with a vengeance, more cynical this time; it breaks down all barriers and fills your spirit with screams that replace words, or with words that make you stutter, with ghosts and shadows that haunt your nightmares by night and feed your neurosis by day. Because when you cut loose from your memory, there are only two choices left: either permanently consign it to the deepest depths of Lethe or, if that doesn't work, surrender yourself to this distorted effigy.

At the other extreme are those who choose to anchor themselves in memory, and turn it into something resembling an old treasure chest, where they keep the clock of their former existence, which stopped ticking long ago, safe. In this case, memory resembles a precious embalmed body: it becomes representative of the golden age, a golden age that never even existed, and never will exist. Those who preserve the past in this way are often regarded as heroes, because they resist change. The truth is that devotees of this brand of memory are nothing more than failed heroes, because they were too frightened or because they simply withdrew from a present that was too painful for them, to seek comfort in an idealized version of the past.

Then there are those immigrants who choose to preserve a paradigmatic relationship with memory. They are not its prisoners but they don't try to eradicate it either. They do not experience their origins as either a stigma or as a protective shield. Memory in their case is not one smooth continual tradition full of nostalgia for roots and scents, a clock stopped and incompatible with the present. This is no marmoreal memory but a part of yourself which is constantly changing. It's the vaulting pole that helps the immigrant live through change with greater honesty and decency and, if possible, with greater wisdom. "I met pain along the way, pushing me further and further along"—the lines of a song the Marseilles immigrants sing. This encounter with pain, pushing us forward all the time, is the human condition par excellence. And the way this encounter is narrated is memory itself.

30

I heard shouting in Albanian, "The ambassador's here! The ambassador's here!" People came rushing out of the warehouse. A van drew up close by us. A white-haired, white-bearded, white-mustached man in his fifties with an aristocratic air got out. He was followed by a woman, and then two young men. One was holding a television camera, the other was carrying something else, possibly a microphone. Our speculations were not entirely unfounded, it seemed; some people had arrived, granted, none of them the candidates we had shortlisted earlier. The white-haired man with the aristocratic demeanor was neither the American nor the British ambassador, nor a big NATO general but a Greek filmmaker called Christos.

Christos had come to document the tragic influx of Albanian immigrants into Greece. He asked if any of us could speak English, and the driver and codriver immediately grabbed me by the arms and carried me across to him, almost airborne. "Tell him what we've been through here," shouted the Albanians around me. "Tell him that the police treat us like animals, they don't give us any food, and don't let us do anything, not even take a piss." A lot more than that was said but those were some of the few phrases I could pick out from all the noise in this tragic place. I don't know what I told Christos. Even today I can't say for sure what the hell it was I told him. All I can remember is that he took me to one side while his two assistants were filming inside the warehouse. The police, observing the zeal with which they were working, reverted to their former grim expressions.

Christos and I started talking about Albania. He was very familiar with Ismail Kadare's work and told me that almost all of Kadare's books had been translated into Greek. Then he looked around at everyone and appeared shocked at the utter misery he saw before him. "You know, I actually believe in communism," he said. I said nothing. There was a pause, and then he said, "What were you doing for fifty long years? Nothing?" I looked him in the eye and then motioned at the crowd with a tilt of my head. "You can see for yourself what we were doing."

The truth is that if someone had seen us Albanians there in Filiates, they would have thought that we'd just been liberated from a concentration camp: the dull colors of our clothes, the shades of gray and black favored by the regime; the undernourished faces that had something wild about them, exacerbated by the cold; the hunger and exhaustion of the past few days; that vacant stare, the same vacant stare of the orphan or of someone who has failed utterly, been defeated utterly.

"Do you want to come with me to Athens?" Christos asked me suddenly. "What would I do in Athens?" I asked him. "Find a job— you know so many languages, you're bound to find something, maybe with a paper. You can stay with me till you've learned some Greek."

I thought I was dreaming. A stranger, someone we'd imagined to be the American ambassador, the British ambassador, and a big NATO general, was offering to put me up in his home. I was desperate to escape the chaos, the misery and the discomfort of the warehouse, and every atom of my being was yearning for a lifeline, some means of moving on now that I had crossed over into the world-beyond-the-borders, a helping hand, just enough to get me on my feet. I said yes at once.

Christos told me to wait, and I saw him walk up to the policemen. It was already dark and the big floodlight had already come on. About ten minutes later he was back telling me that they wouldn't allow him to take me to Athens without getting the go-ahead from the mayor. "I'll be back tomorrow and I'll talk to the mayor," he promised. My instinct told me that if I didn't get away that night, he might not find me there the next day. "Tomorrow will be too late," I answered. He took me by the arm and this time we both went over to the policemen to try to persuade them. I could tell that Christos was trying to butter them up, but from what I could make out, he wasn't getting very far. One of them started prodding me in the back of the neck with his truncheon, repeating the question, "Musulman? Musulman?" My terrified answer, "Not Muslim. Atheist," which I'd hoped would soften him a little, apparently went over his head because he kept on repeating the word, but this time without a question mark: "Musulman. Musulman."

At some point, taking advantage of the relative disturbance being caused, Christos led me off again and took me to one of his assistants, Grigoris. They spoke briefly and Grigoris nodded, as though in response to some secret code, took hold of my arm, and dragged me off. We passed two or three policemen, who at first went for me, but Grigoris managed to get them off by repeating certain words, the same words all the time. He put me in the van and told me to sit at the back and keep out of sight, handed me a blanket (I wasn't sure if this was intended to keep the cold out or to keep me hidden). The rest of the crew soon appeared and hurried into the van and started the engine. We stopped after only a few seconds. More policemen, talking to Christos, but they eventually let us on our way.

I soon digested the fact that this was my second escape. I'd escaped from the warehouse at Filiates. Grigoris told me it was OK and I could sit up. We drove through the darkness, far away from the policemen. From the window, I caught sight of a human caravan walking through the night—my fellow countrymen, having crossed the border into Greece. There, surrounded in darkness, they looked like weary shadows walking *without direction, like ghosts roaming around in the night, briefly illuminated by the headlights of the van. It was then when I felt a river of tears rushing down my throat and I broke into sobs.*

It was January 22, 1991, I think. That's more or less how my life in Greece began.

Epilogue

This tale is not typical of border stories: it comes to an abrupt halt where most of them just keep going without ever reaching the end. Tales of monstrous, visible borders such as the borders of totalitarianism and tales of the invisible, psychological borders experienced in a foreign country rarely reach a conclusion. It was never my intention to tell you the story of my life; what I wanted to tell you about was my illness, Border Syndrome, a condition you won't find documented in any manual of recognized psychological disorders. It's not like agoraphobia, vertigo, depression. And it's not like any physical disease spread by a virus, but that doesn't make me any less of a carrier—maybe just a carrier with low levels, as the doctors are fond of describing carriers of hepatitis whose organs have developed enough antibodies to keep the deadly march of the virus in check. Nevertheless, Border Syndrome is just as pernicious as the hepatitis virus because you can never truly get rid of it. It just sits there, in a latent state, wedged between time and space, wedged between your body and the gaze of others, ready to strike at any moment and take possession of your memories, your silence, the expression in your eyes, your spleen, your smile, your passion and your life. It's then that you start to experience your body and your face and your origins as a burden. You long to be free of it all, if only for just a second, for as long as it takes to cross the borders—if only for that long. Unlike all those self-satisfied people who scream and shout, asserting "the right to be different," what you crave more than anything is the right to be exactly the same as everyone else. You long to go unnoticed, to be invisible. But you know that can never be more than a fantasy—Border Syndrome is hardly the stuff of fairytales. It tends to affect daydreamers, daydreamers who fight tooth and nail to maintain a grip on reality, who fight tooth and nail to overcome both kinds of borders: the visible and the invisible. To work out how much you are at risk of contracting the Border Syndrome virus, all you need to do is remember which side of the border you were born on.

As a carrier of Border Syndrome, I have to confess to having a dream: a dream of a world without immigrants. Don't get me wrong—I love traveling; most sufferers of Border Syndrome do. If you never get out from inside yourself, from your body, your ennui, then you can be pretty confident of lifelong immunity from Border Syndrome. I'd simply prefer people to travel in the real sense of the word, to go traveling, like tourists do, like students do, like bohemians do. To travel like people who have lost their way looking for paradise or like those who have found their own Ithaca through some absurd twist of fate—to travel with dignity. I do not want people to travel in the way that so many Germans, Irish, Italians, and Greeks once traveled, and the way so many Albanians, Afghans, Iranians, Somalis, Mexicans, and so many others are forced to travel today. Because being a migrant by definition puts you in a position of weakness. And in this world, the weak are never treated with respect. They might be pitied, but they are never respected. I remember how in the early days in Athens just after I had crossed the borders, I was walking down the road quietly whistling the lyrics of a song I'd just learned: *I walked through the night / not knowing a soul / and not a soul / not a soul / knew me.* It's one of Mikis Theodorakis's songs. It wasn't written about immigrants, but it does capture the feelings of all those who have at some point experienced true loneliness and have tasted the fear of defeat—sufferers of Border Syndrome, in other words.

I have a dream—I have a dream of a world in which there are no immigrants. But such a world is not feasible, because a world without immigrants would have to be a world free of tyranny; a world free of poverty; above all a world free of the desire that people have to take control of their own destiny. A world free of immigrants and free of migration would be a much duller world than the world we know today. At the same moment that I yearn for a world devoid of immigrants, I count my blessings that I am an immigrant. In the final analysis, it takes guts; it takes guts to go head to head with borders and start your life again from scratch: with language; street names; people's names—to make this foreign city your own. Being a thoroughbred immigrant means acknowledging the power of the will, and coming to terms with the outrageous tricks of fate and to understand that the greatest human virtue is the ability to adapt and change and has nothing to do with who you are descended from, and to realize that the secret of success is at once simple and complicated: never to tire of life.

That I am sitting in Berlin writing these lines is due to a simple twist of fate, one that occurred several years after the events that I narrate in this book took place. I'm on Bernauer Strasse, looking across at what's left of the Berlin Wall. A couple of tourists are sitting next to me, experiencing the whole thing on the level of a tourist attraction, as an interesting historical fact. To me it's as though I am looking at a small piece of the skeleton of the monster that once shut me away in his cell, forbidding any contact with the world beyond the borders; I will always carry the ghost of this monster inside me, wherever I go, however widely I travel, however many borders I cross. A mere few meters away from the skeleton of the monster I can see an advertisement for a mobile phone company, urging passersby to enjoy each and every moment of this short life in a world that is getting smaller and smaller every day—a world in which there are no more borders and no more walls. I absentmindedly flick the pages of my passport inside my jacket pocket. The impenetrable borders and the murderous walls of the Cold War are a thing of the past. Borders and walls live on for the most part inside our pockets. They are the passports we carry. I become aware of this each time I stand at a passport control, because at these checks, there are two categories of people: bearers of "cool passports" and everybody else—people holding "bad passports." If you've got a "cool passport," you've got nothing to worry about. Borders are nothing more than invisible lines, a trick of the imagination, geographical lines as translucent as the light of the Mediterranean. Having a "bad passport," on the other hand, changes everything. It means you have Border Syndrome, and every crossing you make becomes an unforgettable incident, an event on your existential calendar. And the more borders you encounter, the more determined you become to cross them.

I still belong to the "bad passport" group. Greek passports once belonged to the "bad" group but are now part of the "cool" group. I haven't got one. I don't know if I'll ever be given one, so for the time being I'm traveling on my bad one, crossing borders with it. Who knows, it might become "cool" one day. I hope so. The face of the immigration officer checking a "cool" passport usually looks very relaxed and very human. But the expression of the officer checking a "bad passport" is usually very suspicious. He looks at you. He looks at you again. He asks you questions. He asks you outrageous questions. And you give very plausible answers. He asks you the most outrageous questions once again. And you give him very plausible answers once again, waiting for the stamp to fall so that you can get across to the other side of the border, to the other side of the world. When you carry a "bad" passport, borders revert to type; they become what they used to be and what they always will be—miserable places. There are some border posts and customs checkpoints in which the immigration officer is himself the son of immigrants. His parents too had crossed on a "bad passport," or had perhaps stowed away on a train or in the darkness of a boat. Perhaps they tore up their passports so that they wouldn't be deported. And he, born here to parents who at some point arrived from somewhere else, is now checking other people's "bad passports," people who perhaps have the same passion to get to the other side of the border, to emigrate, to put down roots here so that someday their own children might be able to carry a "cool passport" in their pockets. Carriers of Border Syndrome are constantly changing their place of birth, name, and country. However, the way they keep their gaze fixed on the borders, and the way the borders return their gaze, remain unchanged through the ages. And that's because the world keeps turning and then comes full circle. Sometimes it makes progress, breaking down old borders and establishing new ones, irrespective of which side of the borders you find yourself on. In the final analysis, we are all immigrants, armed with a temporary residence permit for this earth, each and every one of us incurably transient.

Author's Note

A Short Border Handbook is part autobiography, part fiction, its heroes both real and invented. It could not have been written without the help of several people, most of them anonymous, who related their own border experiences to me, especially the women immigrants who were generous enough to share their often tragic stories. During the writing of this book, other writers and their works proved inspirational, particularly Zeese Papanikolas and his *Buried Unsung: Louis Tikas and the Ludlow Massacre*; Tsvetan Todorov's *Les abus de la memoire,* as well as newspaper articles by Tahar Ben Jelloun on the subject of immigration. Special thanks go to my mother and brother, to Ilira, to the Internet— and to fortuity.

Gazmend Kapllani
Athens, January 2009

Notes

1 Korçë is a town in southern Albania, close to the Greek border. Kalabaka is a town in the north of Greece, close to Thessaloniki.

2 Kakavia is the main checkpoint on the Greek-Albanian border.

3 Gjirokastër is a city in the south of Albania.

4 Zeese Papanikolas, *Buried Unsung: Louis Tikas and the Ludlow Massacre*, University of Nebraska Press, 1991.

5 "Oh! Nightingale, I have vowed / To find out your nest, double-crosser / Grab you and throw you in the river / Drown you there because our girls lie awake at night because of you, you flirt / You twist, be"

A Conversation with Gazmend Kapllani

You begin (and end) *A Short Border Handbook* by drawing attention to what you call "Border Syndrome" —a hard-to-explain condition not included in any "list of recognized mental disorders." Is this generally understood (especially by immigrants themselves) to be something that many immigrants suffer from, whether named in some manner or not? Did you coin the term or did you encounter it somewhere? Is the condition static or does it change with the times?

There are writers who "owe," so to say, their literary obsessions to their imagination. There are others who owe them to their personal experiences. I belong to the second category. Coining the literary metaphor "Border Syndrome" was, for me, like giving a name to an obsession that has shaped my entire life. I have lived half of my life under totalitarianism and the other half as an immigrant. I was born during the Cold War, when the Iron Curtain divided Europe in two. By the way, I believe that the tragedies of the twentieth century in Europe cannot be fully understood without knowing the history of its borders, fences, and walls.

I was born in Stalinist Albania, a tiny country that was isolated from the rest of the world for half a century by means of terrifying borders and walls. For me and my generation borders and walls mean madness, xenophobia, and terror. And they also mean a longing to cross them.

When communism collapsed I crossed the borders to Greece as a refugee. There I had to deal—this time around —with invisible borders: the foreign language I wanted to conquer, having my papers in order to be recognized as a human being. I was seen as an undesirable when I was a penniless foreigner and I faced hostility and envy when I became a successful immigrant.

No wonder, then, that borders constitute one of my main literary obsessions.

You write, "Those who have never experienced the urge to cross a border, or who have never experienced rejection at a border, will have a hard time understanding us." In writing this book, were you motivated more, at least initially, by a desire to broaden public understanding of Border Syndrome or to chronicle your own experience and those of people you knew?

The voice of the storyteller in my book is rather timid. He belongs to the so-called "first generation" of immigrants. He has experienced borders under totalitarianism and he has faced a lack of understanding and rejection as an immigrant. He is not simply telling a story: he is making a public confession. And he's afraid that many out there, in the imaginary audience, won't be able to understand what he is talking about.

As a writer, though, I wrote this book mostly for those who have never experienced a rejection at the border or have never felt that strange state of mind called the "Border Syndrome."

A Short Border Handbook is both the story of one immigrant's personal journey and a handbook of sorts to describe the general experience shared by all immigrants. You balance these two elements deftly— devoting a portion of each chapter to the story of the protagonist (you, with fictional elements woven in) and another to the immigrant experience as a whole. Why did you opt for this narrative approach?

Let me tell you the story behind this book—which is also my first novel, even if its dual nature leads publishers to categorize it as nonfiction. I started writing it as a long essay that would be strictly based on my personal memories of crossing the border after the collapse of communism. In the course of writing, though, fictional characters popped up in my mind and they drove me to places and meditations that I could have never predicted. They set me free, in the sense that I could travel beyond the narrow horizon of my personal experiences. My personal memoirs were vital to the writing of this book, but at the same time, thanks to my fictional characters—"Sex Boy," for example—I went way beyond my personal story. That's the moment that the book evolved into these two parallel voices. The first voice tells the story of border-crossing, of the journey itself. The second voice is a meditation upon the immigrant journey.

In the second half of many of the chapters, you use the second person perspective—addressing the reader as "you"—to identify the "immigrant." Was the purpose of this choice to allow the reader to some extent imagine him or herself in the place of the immigrant?

As I said before, the parallel narrative is a meditation upon the immigrant journey. I feel that the second voice, far more than triggering empathy for the immigrant, gives the book its integrity. It is, above all, an honest effort to make sense of what the story means—that messy, confused, exciting, painful, and comical experience of crossing borders, of encountering a foreign sky, a foreign language, a foreign culture, as a refugee and an immigrant. It was like putting a mirror in front of myself and my readers at the same time.

Borders play both a literal and metaphorical role in this story. It seems that once immigrants pass into the "world-beyond-the-borders," there are many more metaphorical borders to cross in order to be truly accepted into society—including such difficulties as language and economic barriers. Would you say that there truly isn't a "world-beyond-the-borders" for the immigrant?

We humans live surrounded by borders and boundaries, both visible and invisible. We are engaged in an eternal game of creating borders and boundaries and, at the same time, of inventing the means to subvert them. That's human nature, I guess. But in the case of my storyteller there's an overwhelming, tragicomic presence of borders in his life. He carries within him these two kinds of experiences, which are apparently very different from each other: those of living under a totalitarian regime and of crossing borders as an immigrant. He starts his immigrant journey while the slogan "Tear down that wall!"—from Ronald Reagan's legendary speech in Berlin—is still echoing in his ears; and once he does cross that scary wall, he finds himself surrounded by a crowd that's shouting "Build that wall!"

You also briefly reflect on the history of Greek migration to America—how those immigrants often had to change their names, how they faced challenges in learning a new language, how they experienced xenophobia, and so on. The parallels between that history and the more contemporary history of the Albanian migration to Greece is shocking. Do you think that if more citizens in various countries were aware of their own particular cultural, national, and family histories regarding migration, this might lead to more acceptance regarding immigrants today? It has been noted, after all, that the vast majority of those in America, at any rate, who have called most stridently for curbs on immigration come from families that, not too many generations ago, arrived on that country's shores as refugees or immigrants, in many cases undocumented and unwelcome.

A Frenchman who knew America well, Alexis de Toqueville, said that history is a gallery of pictures in which there are few originals and many copies. That quote has returned to my mind pretty often while reading a lot about the history of immigration and interviewing immigrants from all over the world. A Greek immigrant at the beginning of the twentieth century in America and an Albanian immigrant at the end of the twentieth century in Greece have many more things in common that they have differences.

When I became a well-known journalist in Greece I sometimes highlighted these similarities in my articles. What I saw surprised me: many of my readers were troubled by the comparison. Greece had (and still has) some of the most drastic levels of emigration of any European country. Why, then, did people get so troubled when they were reminded about their past as immigrants, especially by an immigrant like me? I tried to offer some answers. First of all, when Greece became a rich country and people stopped immigrating massively to other countries, there was a cultural tendency to bury into oblivion the painful history of their own immigration. It didn't match the image of the nouveau-riche self.

As you asked though about parallels with America today, I would add something else. Time after time I received messages from some Greeks who had read my articles and who had been themselves immigrants, telling me that comparing Greek immigrants with Albanian immigrants or other refugees was totally wrong. According to them, "the Greek immigrants were different." What they meant was that they were "good immigrants and refugees" as opposed to Albanians and other immigrants in Greece who were considered "bad, violent, lazy immigrants." When I replied to those readers by talking about the historical facts of racism against Greek immigrants in America or elsewhere, where Greek immigrants were seen as violent and lazy, some of these readers would become irrational in their reactions.

It might sound very simple, but at the root of this division—"we, good immigrants" versus "them, bad immigrants"—lies the refusal to recognize the same humanity in the newcomers. New immigrants are considered to be less human or in the worst case, dehumanized.

Last, let me say that the history of immigration, both in Europe and America, is full of examples of old immigrants who turn against the new immigrants, because they feel or fancy that their privileged place in the society or the economy is under threat. This situation becomes explosive, though, if a demagogue tries to turn that hostility into a political movement. It might lead to a sort of "civil war" between different groups of immigrants, between old and new immigrants.

In the epilogue, you refer to a dream the protagonist has in which there would be a world without immigrants. Is a world without immigrants the same thing as a world without borders? If not, what would a world without borders look like?

In my work I see migration as an essential part of the human adventure on this planet, as old as traveling, religion, and poetry. At the same time, I'm not trying to embellish or turn the immigrant's experience into folklore. Being an immigrant often means having an inferior status to natives; it means exposing yourself to the extreme games of fate. As an immigrant you might lose the best of a country and you often have to rely on the kindness of strangers. On the other hand, it takes guts to be an immigrant, to go head to head with borders and start your life from scratch—with language, street names, people's names—to make a foreign city your own. "I met pain along the way, pushing me further and further along"—these are the lines of a song immigrants in Marseilles sing.

I'm not sure how a world without borders would look. What I can say is that my life-long experience with borders has taught me that every time we talk about building strong borders and walls and fences it means that we are angry or frustrated or have badly lost our self-confidence. Before being built on the ground, borders and walls are erected in our minds and souls.

ALSO AVAILABLE FROM
NEW EUROPE BOOKS

In this piercing and resonant debut novel, a young
Bosnian Muslim refugee finds a new home in America—
until the aftermath of 9/11 tests him as never before.

978-0-9973169-0-2

"Powerful, eye-opening reading
for everyone." —*Library Journal*

"Madrygin's harrowing, compelling
debut will live long in the reader's
memory. . . . Deeply informative
and moving, it will spark debates
regarding American foreign policy."
—*Booklist*

"In Madrygin's gripping debut,
the horrors of war give way to
the challenges of carving out a
life in a hostile country."
—*Publishers Weekly*

OTHER TITLES

Ballpoint: A Tale of Genius and Grit, Perilous Times, and the Invention that Changed the Way We Write. 978-0-9825781-1-7

The Essential Guide to Being Hungarian: 50 Facts & Facets of Nationhood. 978-0-9825781-0-0

The Essential Guide to Being Polish: 50 Facts & Facets of Nationhood. 978-0-9850623-0-9

Illegal Liaisons. 978-0-9850623-6-1

Keeping Bedlam at Bay in the Prague Café. 978-0-9825781-8-6

Once Upon a Yugoslavia. 978-0-9000043-4-9

Petra K and the Blackhearts. 978-0-9850623-8-5

The Wild Cats of Piran. 978-09900043-0-1

The Upright Heart. 978-0-990043-8-7

Voyage to Kazohinia. 978-0-9825781-2-4

New Europe Books

Williamstown, Massachusetts

Find our titles wherever books are sold,
or visit www.NewEuropeBooks.com for order information.

ABOUT THE AUTHOR

Gazmend Kapllani, the author of three books, teaches creative writing and European history at Emerson College and was previously a fellow at Harvard University's Radcliffe Institute and a writer-in-residence at Wellesley College. He has held presentations at numerous colleges and universities including the University of Michigan, Columbia University, Brown University, Harvard University, Wellesley College, and Bennington College. Born in 1967 in Albania, he crossed the mountainous border into Greece on foot in 1991. In Greece he worked as a builder, a cook, and a kiosk attendant while earning a doctorate in political science and history at Athens University. For more than ten years he was a columnist for the leading Greek daily *Ta Nea*. *A Short Border Handbook*, inspired by his own experience as an immigrant and written in Greek, was a bestseller in Greece and translated into several languages. Kapllani's other books include the novels *My Name is Europe* (2010, Greece; 2013, France) and *The Last Page* (2012, Greece; 2015, France).

ABOUT THE TRANSLATOR

Anne-Marie Stanton-Ife is a translator of Modern Greek and Norwegian fiction and theater. Notable translations include Henrik Ibsen's *John Gabriel Borkman* and *When We Dead Awaken* (Penguin Classics, 2014) and a biography of Vidkun Quisling (CUP, 1999). Among the Greek authors she has translated are Sergios Gakas, Andreas Staikos, and Vangelis Hatziyannidis. Her translation of Hatziyannidis's *Four Walls* (Marion Boyars, 2006) was shortlisted for the Independent Foreign Fiction Prize, 2007, while her translation of Gazmend Kapllani's *A Short Border Handbook* (Portobello, UK, 2009) was runner-up in the Society of Authors 2012 translation prize for Greek.